The Observer's Reality
A Metaphysics Book

No. 0 - Hubble space telescope deep field galaxies

Printed by: CreateSpace, An Amazon.com Company
• Available from Amazon.com and other retail outlets
ISBN-13: 9780692866856

The Observer's Reality

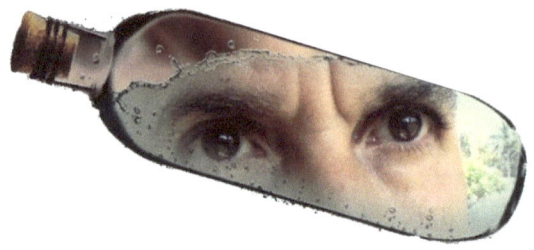

No. 1 – Filtered – Bias – Modulated views

A Metaphysics Book

No. 1a - The observer's location in the galaxy

Author's Biniverse Binary Theory

Look, see, observe, and then analyze…….

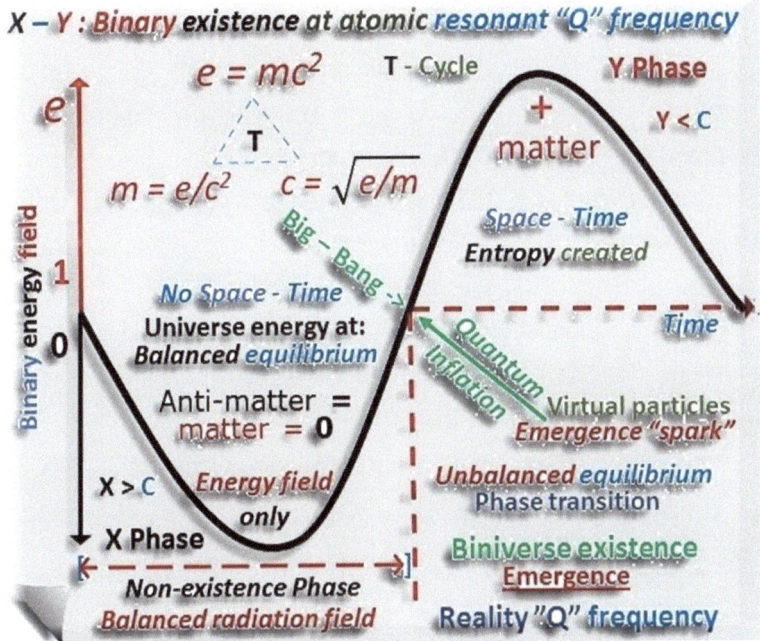

No. 2 Biniverse Graph - Energy – Space – Time
(Ref. Albert Einstein *Theory of Relativity).*
Ref. pages: 111, 113, 119, 122, 126.

By: RAZ Jr.

August 17, 2008

Colophon

The Observer's Reality

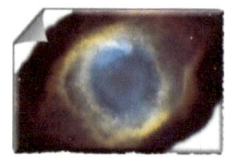

No. 3 – "The Eye of God" constellation

Copyright information: NASA web site content photo images, or data in any format - *Generally are not copyrighted.* As per NASA, you may use this material for educational or informational purposes, including photo collections. This general permission extends to personal web pages. Please ref. page 134 – Credits.
Ref. https://www.nasa.gov/multimedia/guidelines/index.html

Art frame warping, recoloring, differentiated editing was done by the author to all graphic work included.

<u>Nonidentical artwork</u> exists at any public domain sites that requires graphics permissions.

Disclaimer: Be aware that this informative and educational metaphysics book does not contain pictorials, photos, or attachments from any free royalty public domain websites. But hereby also be notified that before taking any commercial actions for monetary purposes based on any of the enclosed book material, artwork documentation, and, or enclosed book information, it should be verified to properly comply, and be authorized by the respective author if required.

Ref. *royalty free clip art and graphics.org* - publicdomainvectors.org
And many other *royalty free clip art and graphics* websites etc.

Printed by: CreateSpace, An Amazon.com Company
• Available from Amazon.com and other retail outlets
ISBN-13: 9780692866856

Dedication

No. 4 – Full Moon

This informative book on metaphysics is dedicated to my dear sweet wife, and my two kind daughters, both of my parents, my brothers, sisters, my closer and distant relatives, friends, esteemed sharp co-workers, and finally also to my extended human family members that are hereby willing to take this research trip with me in the search for knowledge and for answers to some myths, legends, or mysterious phenomena of intriguing puzzles tackled by this new radical metaphysics book about our reality.

No. 5 – Moonlighting

Most of all, I wrote this book in the memory of
my late father: "Zapathousky"
(4/28/26 - 8/17/08)

Acknowledgments

I want to express my most sincere appreciation to my two daughters for all their assistance in the preparation of this whole manuscript. For their constructive criticism of my 2nd language English grammar that gave them a fit.

No. 6 – My Kids - In addition, I would like to extend a special thanks to my wife for sharing her sense of humor, and some laughs during our discussions of this book. She was very helpful during the early programming phase of this undertaking, and was a source of positive motivation to take on this challenge throughout the whole project.

No. 7 – My Wife

I also will like to thank all the members of my close family, and friends for their numerous valuable inputs, and encouragements during this project. Their good sense of humor and feedback on ideas helped a lot in preparing the manuscript and prevented this from becoming an encyclopedia-sized technical book.

I tried to keep the information as compact as possible knowing that it may affect the clarity, but compromised to try to keep the book around 130 pages.

Dear reader, I hope that you enjoy the myriad of information I put together for your reading pleasure, and for expanding your search for answers as you go into your own explorations and journey of your life.

Table of Contents

Title	Page

Sub-title page 2
Author's Biniverse Binary Theory……………….....3
Colophon 4
Dedication.. 5
Acknowledgments... 6
Table of Contents 7,8,9
Definitions - Terms & Abbreviations 15
List of Illustrations 10,11,12,13,14, 15
Frontispiece.. 16
Epigraph... 17
Foreword... 21
Abstract.. 22
Preface 25

Introduction... 27
Prologue... 29
Chapter I: The biniverse "auto-creation" 31
from 0 to 1 or (- to +) quantum energy inflation phase transition theory. Ref. Biniverse graph.

Chapter II: Initial biniverse matter propagation…….37
during the auto-chaos entropy, and creation transition phase

Chapter III: Solar systems, Planets, Moons, &………   43
the formation of Earth

Chapter IV: Creation of minerals, clay…………….. 47
crystals, organic, materials, vegetation, and Earth-life biology.

Table of Contents

Title	Page
Chapter **V**: DNA based organic life............ of human's biology	56
Chapter **VI**: The temporary illusion of......... existence & its end.	65

Universal life: Is a biniversal emergent process.

Chapter **VII**: The need of our spiritual.......... life experiences	69
Chapter **VIII**: The human physical brain.......... and the virtual 4-D mind sensory illusions	73
Chapter **IX**: The philosophical existence.......... illusion of our reality	80
Chapter **X**: Our temporary existence............. the reality of life and death	84
Chapter **XI**: The Brain: The receptor &............ decoder of our own sensory-perceived 4-D reality	94
Chapter **XII**: Summary and conclusions............ to the mysteries of our existence, and philosophical probabilities for solutions to some of the mysterious life's puzzles.	99
The End...... & ... The Beginning............	106
Miscellaneous notes ....19, 20, 24, 30, 36...42	
Miscellaneous notes...............44, 46, 64, 68, 72.. 79	
Miscellaneous notes ....83, 93, 98, 119,..122	

Table of Contents

Title	Page
Epilogue	107
Afterword	108
Conclusion	109
Who are we? Findings and discussion of different mysteries.	
Postscript	111
Glossary	112, 113, 114
Glossary	115, 116, 117, 118
Bibliography	120
Resources	121
References	123, 124, 125
Postface	126
Appendix A	127
Appendix B	128
Appendix C	129
Book keywords	130
Index	131, 132.. 133
Credits	134
About the Author	135
Author's Notes	136
The End	137

List of Illustrations

Figure No.	Title Description	Page
0	Hubble space telescope deep field galaxies	1
1	Filtered – Bias – Modulated views	2
1a	The observer's location in the galaxy	2
2	Biniverse Graph Energy–Space-Time	3
3	"The Eye of God" constellation	4
4	Full Moon	5
5	Moonlighting	5
6	My Kids – Acknowledgment	6
7	My Wife - Acknowledgment	6
8	Quantum & Astro-physics reality The Observer's Reality	16
9	DNA Double Helix	17
10	The human cell	18
10a	The human cell structure details	19
2a	Biniverse Graph Energy–Space-Time	21
11	Quantum Particle Physics	22
12	Particles Accelerator Collisions	22
13	Brain Art	23
14	Particles Interaction	25
15	Particles Collisions	26
16	The Observer	27
17	Welcome to Reality	28
18	Eye - mindful observation	28
19	Brain view	29
20	Binary Graph-Energy–Space-Time	30
21	Particle's Collisions Interaction	32
22	3D Biniverse composition view	33
23	2D Biniverse view	34
24	Hydrogen <u>unbalanced</u> present biniverse	35

List of Illustrations

Figure No. Title Description	Page
25- Biniverse phase transition expansion	37
26- Biniverse galaxies & new matter formation	38
27- The expanding biniverse distribution	39
28- The infinite biniverse emerged out of quantum chaos	40
29- The Milky Way galaxy	40
30- Planets celestial body classification	41
31- Milky Way galaxy	41
32- Solar system planets view	43
33- Earth's view	44
34- Milky Way & Earth's location	45
35- Earth evolutionary chaotic formation	45
36- Earth's Natural Minerals	47
37- Periodic Table of Elements	48
38- Biniverse dynamic chaotic evolution	49
39- Life in the Milky Way galaxy	50
40- Earth's life evolution	51
41- Initial marine life evolution	52
42- Initial marine vegetation	53
43-43a - Initial life single cell organisms	54
44- Laboratory life creation experiment	55
44a- Stanley Miller life creation experiment	56
45- Binary Table 1 - Energy- Space-Time	58
46 – Human cell	59

List of Illustrations

Figure No.	Title Description	Page
47-	Human Body	59
48-	Homo Sapiens	59
49-	Life Evolution	60
50-	Chromosomes	61
51-	DNA	61
52-	3D Proteins	62
53-	DNA - RNA Molecules	62
54-	Human Chromosomes	63
55-	Microscope	65
56-	Telescope	65
57-	The observer's human body	66
58-	Technology tools	67
59-	A-B-C Dependency needs	68
59-	Dependency Needs	69
60-	Brain Galaxy	69
61-	Family	70
62-	Spirituality	70
63-	Reality	70
64-	Chaos	71
65-	Chaos Theory + Life	71
66-	Neuron	73
67-	The Human Brain	73
68-	Human Brain	73
69-	Brain Neuron	74
70-	"Q" Mini-universe	74
71-	Brain Neuron's Mapping	75
72-	The "Q" Brain	76
73-	The "Q" brain is a problem solver	76
74-	The virtual 4-D mind	77

List of Illustrations

Figure No.	Title Description	Page
75-	Mind	78
76-	Consciousness	78
77-	The physical brain, virtual mind	78
78-	Illusions vs. reality	80
79-	The Mind	81
80-	Auto-Blood Cell Analyzer Technology	82
80a-	Modern Technology Glucose Meters	83
81-	Humans	84
82-	DNA	84
83-	Proteins	85
84-	Cells	85
85-	Human Cell	85
86-	Human Cells	86
87-	Gene's Info. Xfer.	86
88-	DNA	87
89-	DNA Double Helix	87
90-	Universal Life Transfer	88
91-	DNA Genetic Transfer	88
92-	Virus Life Forms	89
93-	Death Light Tunnel	89
94-	Atomic Reality	90
95-	Quantum Reality Energy	90
96-	Half empty vs. half full glass	91
97-	The cat - dead or alive	91
98-	Chess Board	92
98a-	Chess game board set-up	93
98b-	Chess clock	93
99-	"Q" Brain	94
100-	Brain Neurons	94
101-	Universe – Biniverse	95
102-	A virtual view of the known Universe	96

List of Illustrations

Figure No.	Title Description	Page
103-	Brain Neuron's Mapping	97
104-	Brain Internal View	97
105-	Brain Neuron's View	99
106-	Earth's Internet Connectivity View	100
107-	Brain Activity View	101
108-	Brain Connectivity View	102
109-	Cell Communications	103
110-	Brain Mind Awareness Activity	104
111-	Brain Mind Awareness	105
112-	The "Q" Brain-Mind Observer	105
113-	The Beauty of Nature	106
114-	Database's complex structure	107
115-	Atomic Particles	108
116-	String Theory Math	108
117-	Optional Possibilities	109
118-	Energy -Time & Space	110
117-	Universe Distribution	110
2b-2c	Biniverse Graph Energy–Space-Time	111

Glossary

120-	Life Timeline	114
121-	Biniverse Graph Energy–Space-time	116
122-	Biniverse Expansion	117
123-	Life Evolution	118

About the Author

125-	The Observer	135
126-	The Observer's Skull	135
127-	Multi-Layer Glucose Meter PCB	135
CRD -	Multi-Layer Glucose Meter PCB	136
MISC -	Multi-Layer PCB's Designs	137

List of Illustrations

Figure No.   Title Description   Page

Tables

45   Binary Table 1 - Energy- Space-Time   58

Definitions: Terms & Abbreviations

Approx.: Approximately or ~
Biniverse: The binary quantum "universe". Ref. Fig. 2
Binary math system: Base 2 - Only digits 0 & 1 are used
DB: Database – P&V is a software DB application
4D: Four-dimensional existence = 3 Space + 1 Time
Emergence: Materialization process that is central in theories of integrative levels and complex systems. Ex. World cultures, life from chemistry, universe/biniverse.
Fractals: Fragmented geometric shape that are a never-ending pattern of a reduced/size copy of the whole.
Inflation: Surge, rise, upturn, increase, gain, growth
MTBF: Minimum time before failure
PCB: Printed circuit board (Electronic design)
"Q": Quantum – Physical quantity – Quantum theory
Radiation energy: Waves, particles, atomic rays
Ref.: Reference
Singularity: Infinite small density point in space-time
Sinewave: Mathematical curve that describes a smooth repetitive oscillation. It is named after the function sine.
www: World Wide Web – Internet connectivity

Please ref. to pages 113 to 130: Glossaries, References, Resources, Postface, Appendixes and Book Keywords.

Frontispiece

I want to thank all the readers of this book for being willing to embrace an unfamiliar territory, and to being open to seeing things from a new different angle, perspective, and/or radical out of the box speculative new points of view that in some cases would be very challenging to accept, analyze, or even comprehend.

I also thank you for your patience in trying to understand the different solutions to the mysteries covered in The Observer's Reality book during our own search for knowledge, and answers about true reality, with exciting creative myriad probabilities of life itself.

No. 8 - Quantum & Astrophysics reality

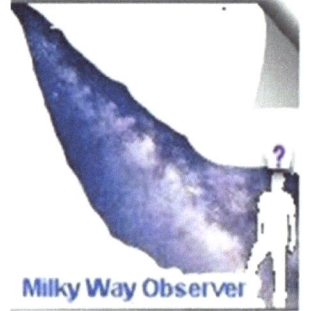

The Observer's Reality

Challenge yourself to come up with your own ideas about every subject of this book. Every possible solution to the puzzles, and mysteries phenomena is hereby given as just a _probability_ that per present scientific knowledge will be 100% accurate in the new multiverse, universe or biniverse theory, and the law of probabilities that provides for new insightful enhanced awareness.

Quantum physics is a tough scientific human reality in which our brave new technological advanced civilization, and Earth's existence depends on its rules.

Epigraph

No. 9 - *DNA Double Helix* - [A ◇ T – C ◇ G]

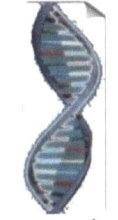
An interesting fact is that at present time the human species are at a new threshold in which we are acquiring the technological genetic knowledge, and scientific advantage to be able to accelerate our very slow, chaotic random and natural evolutionary time consuming process.

The new radical technological epic advances allow modifications to existing living organisms including plants, animals, and our own human genetic code to improve it on as required basis in many new different advantageous ways for the future benefit of humankind.

Some of these new genetic processes are considered controversial, and of course bring with them some social, and moral issues that we will have to tackle as a society at different levels of government with good supervision so that the process is not abused, and/or creates new problems instead of some new answers, improvements, or solutions to some of the existing genetic, and or biological diseases that humans are suffering from at present time including all types of molecular biological virus, and chemicals' cancers being created by our modern civilization factories' chemicals, and daily stress.

The new field of biological genetic engineering seems to offer a new brave world of possible advanced technological scientific medical breakthroughs for the betterment of humans if we are able to work together at a global scale. The positive possibilities seem to be enormous and limitless for the cure of plants, animals, and human misery caused by all types of illness, and diseases plaguing living biological organisms at present time being controlled by our old bio-cellular structures.

No. 10 - The human cell

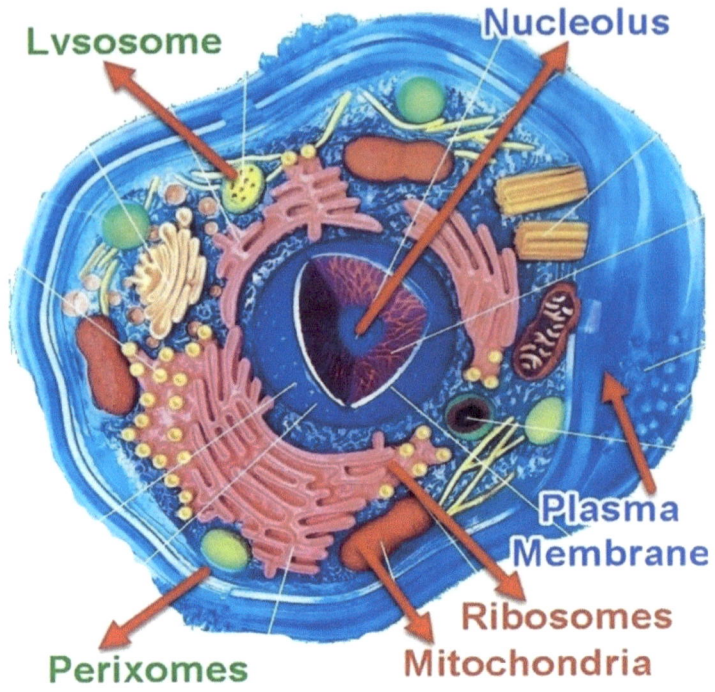

The new CRISPR-Cas9 technology has the potential to allow us to be able to edit the RNA genetic cell genomes structure, thereby allowing us to use the new reprogramming capability of the DNA / RNA in plants, animals, and human embryos to rewire our own cells.

The technology is presently available to control our genetic organic chemistry. But how we use it to modify our own cells in an ethical way is yet to be seen due to its moral, and ethical implications within our present Genomic government restricted and approval systems.

I firmly believe this new innovative technology, and stem cell therapy will help us overcome some of our genetic limitations required to adapt to our changing and challenging ongoing environmental crisis to increase the probabilities for the future survival of our own species.

The Observer's Reality - Miscellaneous notes

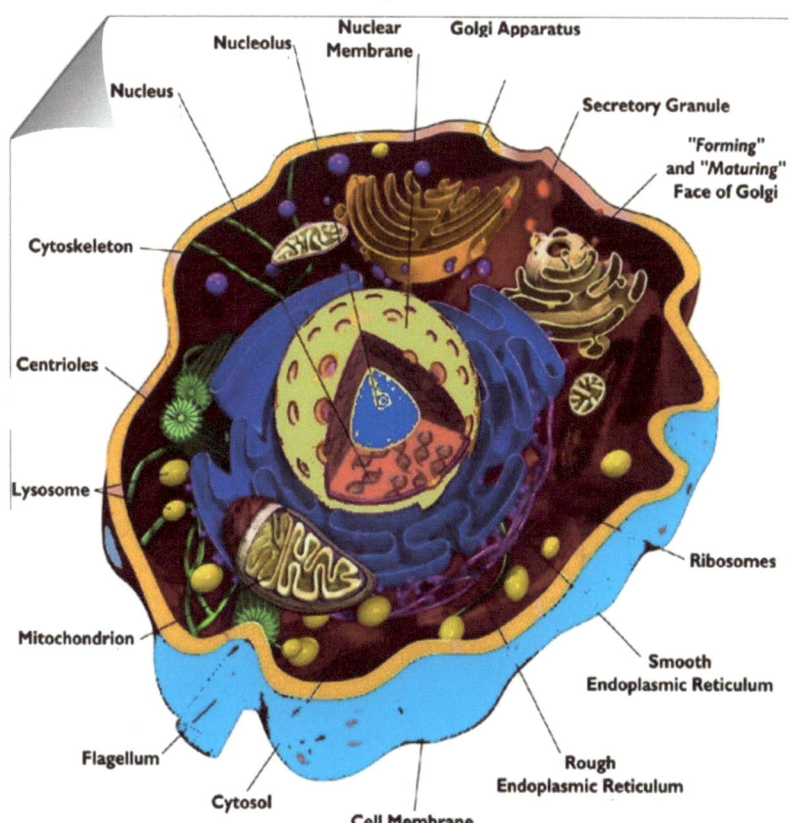

No. 10a - The human cell structure details

Some human cell facts are:

Our bodies contain approx. 75 to 100 trillion cells.

Cells range in size from 1 to 100 micrometers.

Eukaryotic and prokaryotic are primary types of cells.

Prokaryotic single-celled organisms were the earliest most primitive forms of life on earth including bacteria.

Eukaryotic cells have a true nucleus enclosed within a membrane. Plants, fungi, protists and animals are organisms that have eukaryotic cells.

Our bodies have more bacterial cells than human cells

The Observer's Reality - Miscellaneous notes

Notes:

In the previous sections, and the next 5 are special required *brain priming* informative tangent phases before we can tackle Chapter I.

This book is written in a way that 12 chapters are designed to progressively build on each other's related information to help find answers to questions that have mystified humanity for millennia addressing some of life's greatest mysteries eventually reaching a resolution of what our true reality existence is, explained to be understood with the typical layperson's knowledge.

Please read on, and do not worry if now it is not quite clear to understand this new material…. It is just needed preliminary advanced information for the topics that will be covered starting with Chapter I. Give it time, and everything will start to make sense…….

Some human cells reality facts:

Cells have varying life spans. Also, they can commit suicide or kill each other when they become damaged by infections. They are genetically pre-programmed to self-destruct by a process called apoptosis, or by the white blood killer cells that control our body immune systems to protect and keep us healthy on daily basis.

A human cell inability to perform the normal process of apoptosis controlled by the cell **telomeres** will result in uncontrolled cell growth that can become cancerous.

Ref. page 62. Cancer cells.

Foreword

Knowledge is the light that allows us to see into the obscurity of myths, legends, and the dark unknowns.

Before the biniversal radiation energy changed to 100% full hydrogen being the simplest atom. One (+) proton, and one (-) electron, (negative & positive). This initial balanced, symmetrical, binary, radiation energy field was filling an infinite option of a dual probability with equal values that are a binary to exist or not to exist.

Yielding these two options. 1st is to stay as a binary balanced only energy radiation state for eternity. To create a virtual of non-atomic reality. The existence of a perfect balance of 50% matter and 50% anti-matter = -X

The 2nd. option was to experience a "Quantum" moment of *unbalanced energy* with chaotic inflation of expanding emergent perpetual infinite creation of a Biniverse. A universe with unlimited planetary existence as the other option of equal binary quantum energy possibility of the +Y phase as shown on sinewave below.

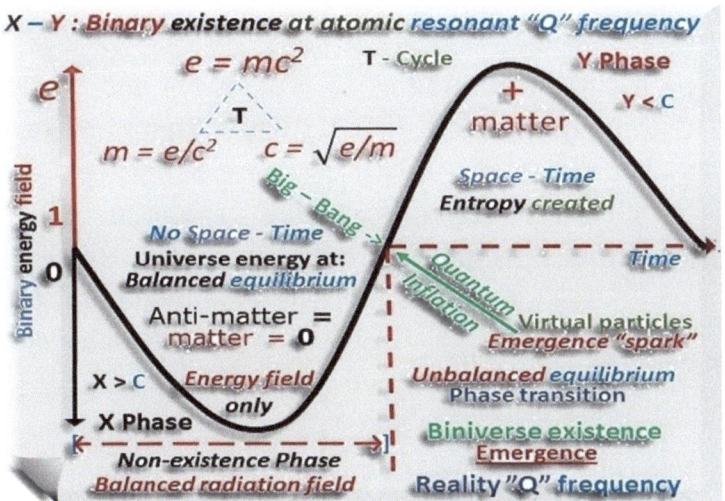

No. 2a Biniverse Graph - Energy – Space – Time
(Ref. Albert Einstein *Theory of Relativity*). Ref. pages 113, 116, 119.

Abstract

No. 11- Quantum Particle Physics

Quantum physics states that the position of an electron in an atom of hydrogen, and any other atom for that matter is unknown, and can be at any place, any time. What if this phenomenon could have been the cataclysm to unbalance the initial universe balanced state, and this also prevents a static non-existence state, so it will start a chaotic creation of the quantum moment of an unbalanced infinite energy field that auto-creates the spontaneous universe inflation emergence sequence as shown per Y phase in the graph.

No. 12 - Particles Accelerator Collisions

A good observation is that quantum math only works with the binary  hydrogen atom. After other heavier denser elements are created by stars, then chaos, and entropy rein all.

This cataclysm was the key *spark* required to get everything in a chaotic motion of initial creation using an infinite energy field of simple atoms of Hydrogen.

The binary probabilities of a previous non-existence phase transition to existence binary quantum, or Big Bang -/+ as in 0 non-existence change to 1= existence, or spontaneous phase transition quantum moment creating time/space in the process at the Big-Bang point.

Later, stars were formed from the 100% hydrogen energy field permeating the whole biniverse. Then as a new creation or new phase, stars converted hydrogen into heavier elements and the new chaotic creation process got into full auto-manufacturing speed mode for billions of years on a constant on-going creation process for approximately 13.77 billion years until present time.

If we use the modern quantum physics multiverse theory, are open, and willing to question previous knowledge, or accept different points of view presented here to the readers, and to reassess previous acquired information living any feelings or human emotions behind, and willing to unlearn some typical accepted equations, then we're ready to go on this research trip.

Note: Please keep in mind that the original non-existence & existence, are two basic quantum physics probabilities that both have the same physical and mathematical quantity values. Therefore, nothing limits them

No. 13 – *Brain Art* – both to be present at the same space-time, in a multidimensional binary interconnected entangled time and space compendium of a binary quantum controlled and initially balanced energy field.

In a binary field both sides need to co-exist at the same time. In the original universe balanced binary system of:
$0 = 1$ mathematically, and Positive = Negative or Physically: Electron (-) = Proton (+) will yield a balanced infinite energy field of the original simple atom of hydrogen. This was a good balanced *probability*. A possible solution to solve the mysterious phenomena or puzzle of initial balanced duality of the binary quantum radiation energy field.

It is also known that given time, *evolution* can be a very *intelligent designer* capable of modifying the most complex living organisms to allow them to thrive, and survive overcoming most environmental adversities, following natural laws that prefers the survival of the fittest, to pass on better genetics to the next new updated generation of species to ensure their future survival.

The Observer's Reality - Miscellaneous notes:

As you will see, all 12 chapters are designed to progressively build on these preliminary *brain priming phases* with new subliminally related information.

Please read on, and do not worry if at this early time your understanding of the presented material is still not yet clear...just keep going....

This is still a special *brain priming phase* presently planting the *seeds* of some deep questions into your subconscious brain using a subliminal neuroplasticity process that will help you find answers to what controls our physical resemblance, and the meaning of life and death among other puzzles.

Relax, and enjoy the provided preliminary necessary information. We are getting closer to Chapter I....

The reality of some types of "love" ....

Love is a "chemical reaction" in our limbic system:

This chemical cocktail of several neurotransmitters and hormone compounds released from the posterior lobe of the pituitary gland causes the amygdala, our feelings and emotional memory control center to overflood.

These neurochemicals such as oxytocin, endorphins, vasopressin, dopamine, and serotonin stimulate brain "desire and reward zones" with an intense rush of pleasure seeking effects. Thereby also triggering the sex hormones, and other neuropeptides that govern these emotional drives such as norepinephrine (adrenalin), male testosterone hormone, or the female estrogen sex hormone. Some love types can be very complicated ☺.

Ref. page 23.

Preface

The Observer's Reality is intended to be a radical book containing synthesis on possible solutions, and or probabilities about philosophical scientific concepts that have captivated the minds of many observers for years.

In our search for answers, we must carefully, observe details to discern the complexity to our limited field of perception and detect the small percentage of the reality that we are capable to perceive with our limited five sensory inputs (i.e., sight, hearing, taste, smell, touch), even with aid of present modern advanced technological instrumentation to help us see *true* reality.

Note: At present time, the known, and/or perceived universe is still approximately 95% in its original form of the most basic binary simple (- N & + P) hydrogen atoms.

No. 14 - *Particles Interaction*

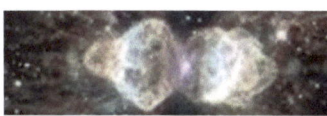

Our perceived reality is generated by vibrations or atomic energy strings fields *(Ref. String Theory)* that pervade all of space at different electromagnetic atomic resonant frequencies in the spectrum of the oscillating universe. One interesting question is: why did life as we know it emerged from these processes? Ref. Page 114.

Why does the universe, the Milky Way galaxy, our solar system, the planet Earth even exist? Why did life evolve on Earth, and why did we come into existence? What are the other opposite possible and or feasible binary options?

And once we undertake this trip down the rabbit's hole, can we get to the bottom of it? If so, then the key question may become not *why*, but <u>*how*</u> was this feasible?

No. 15 - Particles Collisions -

Do you want to go on a logical journey to learn more about these questions? If so, then fasten your seat belt for a *hypothetical trip into my brain* in the search of our true reality.

I hope to share with you questions that capture my imagination. But to get the most of this book, please keep an open mind in reading my various hypotheses. The chapters are designed to progressively build on previous concepts so that readers can use all the pieces presented to help see emerging possible solutions to rationally resolve the phenomena as a series of 12 probabilities.

I believe that fate is partially determined by the Chaos Law. The other possible option does predict that things may be under our own control. I hate to burst your bubble. But the ugly truth is that chaos controls the whole universe *(Sorry, Albert)*. Entropy is part of the universal, or biniversal creation equation as per Y sinewave phase.

Today, physicists and engineers are probing the fundamental structure of the biniverse using powerful particles colliders such as the one operated by CERN (European Council for Nuclear Research). Particles are made to collide together at speeds close to that of the speed of light to emulate how the universe creates new particles. This has been found to occur during collisions of gigantic celestial bodies, which change energy into new atomic matter as per the $m = e/c^2$ formula. Ref. *Higgs Boson* sub-atomic particles.

We will tackle this interesting concept later in the next chapters. As it stands presently in our search for answers to our mysteries. We now have an "empty book" and it needs a lot of answers, so let us go shopping for new elements, galaxies, solar systems, planets, and life in our search for logical answers to our unknown puzzles after the next two preliminary sections are taken care of.

Introduction

This is a brief informative educational *Metaphysics* book with radical controversial new ideas where the author will try to show the reader how from his point of view as an observer of our reality, all the pieces fall into the puzzle. To see the way things fit in, to explain some of the most profound, and fascinating existing old life mysteries of our past, present, and future universe/biniverse.

The reality of existence within binary quantum system fields will be explained as a series of creative alternatives built into 12 chapters with consecutive possible solutions.

From your own, and the observer's perceptions, we both will tackle some of the most intriguing questions that we  humans consider scientific, religious, and life phenomena most popular unknown mysteries, legends, and or **No. 16- The Observer** - mystical dreaded myths during our binary quantum illusion of our own existence on planet Earth

Why this metaphysics reference book is different? In this informative radical book, I am asking the reader not to use *blind faith* and believe the things that we cannot prove right. But to question every one of the observations, and concepts presented by the book author, and to try to find a better answer if possible without a theoretical physicist degree, and or with it. I welcome the observer's different points of view with open minds to allow see reality in a new controversial out of the box radical new way.

I ask the reader to question observations or concepts. To draw alternative theories; the same way scientists try to find flaws in a hypothesis; so, in other words, I want the readers to have an open mind. Consider this book as a *thesis* presented to you on the history of our existence, our perception of reality, the beginning of the universe, formation of galaxies, birth of the solar systems, formation of Earth, and other planets, how evolution created life on it. But an even more interesting question is: <u>how</u> the universe did it? Or what were the other options, if there was even another feasible option? Or possible probability for our binary existence?

Some of the most interesting complex old mysteries will be discussed: existence vs. creation, the universe, the Milky Way galaxy, Earth, life, death, and the scientific evidence that confirms or gives proof of the existence of a divine entity of God. How matter emerged into existence, where are we going? Why do we exist now? How the brain/mind connection creates our reality. Etc.
No. 17 – Reality – Let us get real about it.

Does our existence or absence make any difference to the infinite universe? Did we come from somewhere else? What if there was no planet Earth...? Will humans exist forever? Our sun will not last forever. Are we that important? Or it is just our **egos** that makes us believe other myths, and legends, clouding our perception to prevent us from being able see the true reality of our short existence within our scientific well-known human's limitations to perceive it with our five Q senses.

From the observer's own perspective of our existence, or our perception of a very limited observed, and detected sensory reality we will look for possible clarifications to the unknown puzzles.

Was there a creator of everything...? And if so, do we have a respective description of this fact in an intellectually challenging way to scientifically present a new concept to solve the mystery of the Holy Trinity, or a new description of God from the observer's point of view. Please have an open mind. Remember that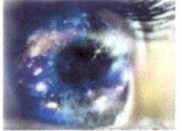
to be mindful is to be present and aware of your mind. **No. 18-Eye**

Please do not pre-judge all the mysteries hypothesis arguments, and or rationale until *The End* after all this controversial radical new informative material is presented as per the observer's own alternate observations, and hypothesis are all described in as much conceivable detail as possible within the limitations of this small, compact book that I put together for the reader's convenience.

I think that all science disciplines, and religious concepts can co-exist without any conflicts, and in fact even better after some of the unknown religious mysteries discussed in this book are solved. I hope the reader agrees with the information presented here as 12 probabilities of possible solutions to the mystery's, phenomena, myths, and or unknowns of this reality research trip.

Prologue

Some of the author's ideas presented in this informative educational Metaphysics, book are daring or to say it mildly very controversial in nature. But they are also the result of some interesting radical new thinking that will challenge the way we see our existence as a creation of everything out of *nothing*, versus accepting the author's speculative idea that it is all just a *Binary Quantum System* with equal probabilities.

A binary energy radiation field existence was always just there…. without needing a formal beginning per se.

In a binary duality probability creation system. It just will be, since non-existence is equal or will have the same mathematical value to existence. Ref. pages 3 &111
No. 19 – Brain view – "*Come in" until...* Ref. page 135

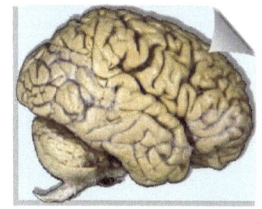

To my own knowledge all connections, or new deductions, are conclusions reached by the author as a derivative process of the science technical research, and personal view analysis that in time yielded possible answers to try and solve all the mysteries described at the end of each chapter in these writings are his own conjectures. They all are also made from actual present human knowledge available as free domain in the www, and presented here as a series of provocative ideas for the benefit of the reader in the human's informative search for answers to the unknown mysteries, and scientific phenomena with a different paradigm's view.

The author does not claim to be the only person with the same radical, logical and/or controversial ideas in The Observer's Reality book. Others, and or even you may also think in this way or have similar ideas. So, let us start on this research trip to see possible solutions…

The Observer's Reality - Miscellaneous notes

We finally got to Chapter I after meeting the different parts needed for a Self-Published book. I am following a book template to meet the book's publishing industry needed standards. This is a special designed book, and previous sections are part of this special book's structure, including the future sections following the end of Chapter XII at pages 106 & 107 to 136 listed below:

Epilogue - Afterword – Conclusion - Who are we? - Findings and discussion of different mysteries – Postscript – Glossaries - Bibliography - Resources - Postface – Appendixes - Book Keywords - Indexes - About the Author, and Author's Notes are all required, and they all complement the book's information that is given in a compressed way to keep this a small book.

For your own benefit please read this book until the end at page 137. Now let us finally start Chapter I.

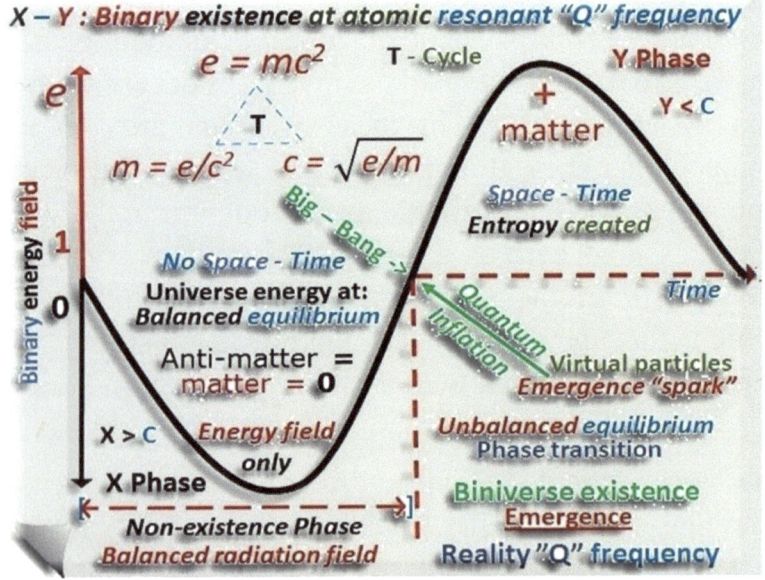

No. 20 - *Biniverse Graph - Energy – Space - Time*

Chapter I

The biniverse "auto-creation" from 0 to 1 or -N to +P quantum energy inflation phase transition theory.

Universe/Biniverse = The binary *quantum* universe

The key question to start this book is not *why* or *who* created the universe, but <u>*how*</u> was it all created?

I will try to simplify the description of the initial process that took place when there was a balanced binary <u>nothing</u> or an infinite universe full of balanced energy of -N = +P field approximately ~13.77 billion years ago (yielding 100% radiation energy). Before an initial quantum phase energy transition *unbalanced* the energy radiation field as per the $E = MC^2$ formula, the hydrogen atom of -N & +P was created as a binary emergence.

A singularity of nothing or a million billion, billion times smaller than a single atom. Or "what if" it was just a binary probability of **0** or **1**. To exist or not to exist produced the phenomenon of "emergence" of the atom of hydrogen. An energy field called a negative electron, and a positive proton (- & +) or an energy field with the same binary probabilities to exist or not everywhere since space - time were initially limited as a pure singularity. Ref. Theory of Relativity. Fig. 20

A balanced initial state of two binary equal probabilities of an infinite nothingness state could produce the **0** to 1 phenomenon of *emergence inflation* of the binary wave cycle creating 100% hydrogen atoms.

This act of coming into appearance, or instantly pop-up into materialization by the emergent manifestation, surfacing to existence by emerging from (- to +) of a **0** to 1 energy field phase transition causing instant inflation.

The emergence of hydrogen energy field into being.

There seems to be a new possibility for us to consider: Now we have an initial infinite full biniverse that just emerged out of an infinite nothingness, and is full of balanced hydrogen atoms (1 electron (-) negative & 1 proton(+) positive) as part of an initial energy *balanced* binary system quantum phase change or a new Biniverse.

No. 21 - Particle's Collisions Interaction

How long do you think this initial condition lasted? Tera seconds? It lasted no time at all! Did time exist? No. Did space exist? No. Both time and space were created during this (- to +) or **0** to **1** Quantum binary energy field phase transition or biniverse emergence pop-into reality.

Well if quantum physics tell us the location of an electron in an atom is unpredictable, the initial balanced condition did not last any time at all. And another emergence therefore also took place creating the initial "small quantum bang moment." Then, chaos, and entropy were also born as per $M = E / C^2$ formula.

This initial *unbalanced* energy field started changing into more complex forms of energy, when millions of stars as neutron, pulsar, hypernovas were formed out of the hydrogen atoms that filled the initial infinite new biniverse 100%. These stars, with their respective black holes at the end of their lives, in turn started the galaxies' process using the newly created unbalanced gravity forces rotating around the respective massive black holes for billions of years creating new atoms, and new matter.

Note: A new conceptual description of balanced Time, Space, and Energy = *Nothing* yielding a supersymmetry binary balanced initial state in which time, and space were possibly confined into a black hole, or a singularity later expanding to the present state of approx. ~70% dark energy, ~25% dark matter, and the visible known atomic universe made up of the balance of approx. ~5% atomic structure as described by the presently accepted scientific particle standard model.

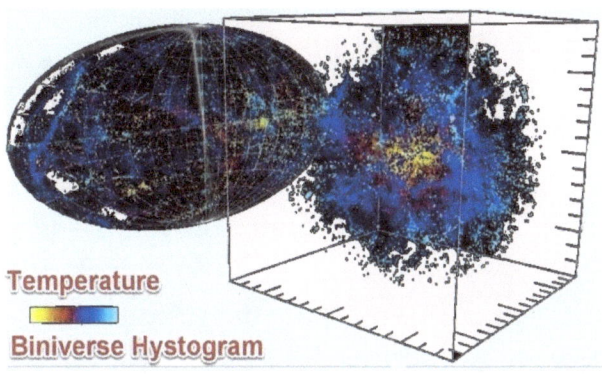

No. 22 - 3D Biniverse Composition View

In other words, a singularity is required to change the perception we presently have of the actual erroneous idea, or the description of this term, since "nothing" is an impossibility, as is non-existence of the known universal energy of the unbalanced infinite binary quantum field, which obviously cannot be full of nothing as shown by the binary graph biniverse sinewave cycle. Ref. page 3.

The universe exists because it has to. There is no other choice! In an initial non-existence and existence binary system of duality. Both probabilities have the same mathematical, and physical values, and therefore they must exist, and non-exist at some universal natural resonant existence frequency of the string energy fields as shown per binary graph page 111 - 2b sinewave cycle.

As we can see, "infinite nothingness" can cause emergence of the hydrogen energy field which was the only *"balanced"* probability of initial (- & +) or 0 & 1 binary radiation system.

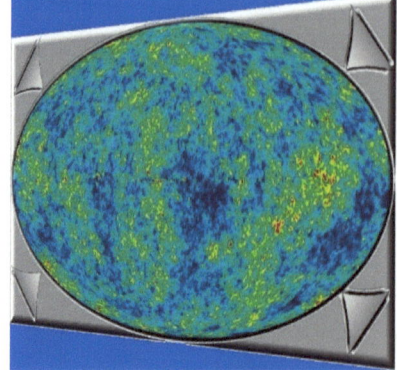

We can also see that initially, this biniverse, or binary universe must have been at some early time 100% full of hydrogen atoms which are the simplest atoms of them all with only (1 Electron (-) Neg. & 1 Proton (+) Pos. - **No. 23- 2D Biniverse View**

We presently know that the materialized visible biniverse is only 5% of the entire universe, and the other invisible 95% is composed of hydrogen. Well, I think this is the right track for trying the re-engineer the whole initial process or energy balanced binary duality system conversion into matter. Ref. $M = E / C^2$ formula.

The binary auto-creation of hydrogen atomic energy field auto-emergence is the root cause of the present chaos, because both options have equal energy field force and repel/attract each other at the same time.

Pos. = Neg., Matter = Anti-Matter, or in other words Existence = Non-Existence at the resonant frequency of quantum creation, and existence of biniversal reality using chaos trying to find the original balanced state.

In particle and quantum physics, scientists wonder how and why sub-atomic particles pop in and out of existence during quantum energy phase transitions of their binary energy fields from 0 to 1. Non-existence to to existence materialization phenomenon occurrence.

This spontaneous phase transition quantum moment allowed the creation of sub-atomic particles to start oscillations, and or rotations getting the new universe in motion, creating space-time and atoms from an energy field of − to +, positive greater than negative, or 1 > 0 binary *unbalanced* energy big-bang, and or inflationary quantum moment. But this binary initial oscillation always existed, so there is not a beginning per se. It always was. It just always will be as the sinewave shows.

Quantum binary non-existence is equal to existence.

No. 24- Hydrogen <u>unbalanced</u> present biniverse

Even though this metaphysics book is written as both informative/educational material, I do not expect the subjects covered to be very comprehensive or easy to digest due to the objective subject matter covered in a radical, and contradictive new ways by challenging answers to the tackled unknown phenomena of the puzzle's solutions. <u>But new chapters will make it easier.</u>

<u>**Summary**</u>**: This mystery puzzle is hereby given a possible solution. Ref. Astrophysics, Cosmology, etc.**

How the universe emerged out of "nothing" probability?

The hydrogen energy unbalanced biniverse <u>emerged</u> out of a binary 0-Neg. to 1+Pos. nothingness, or out of an initial radiation binary energy "Q" field transition.

The Observer's Reality - Miscellaneous notes

Notes:

Book chapters are using subliminal neuroplasticity *brain priming concepts* to help the reader see the pieces of the puzzle falling into their respective place.

Every new chapter will help you to better understand the previous, and the next chapters until all physical reality is explained to your intellectually curious brain.

The more elaborately we encode new memories in our brain, the stronger they will be created. Also, most memories tend to disappear within minutes unless we repeat the new information we want to learn.

Please read on, and do not worry if now is not clear to understand the new hypotheses material, since every keyword is worthy of its own book to explain it.

Stay with it…. You will be glad you did.

FYI – *Astronomical spectroscopy* can be used to find the atomic chemical composition using the spectrum of electromagnetic visible light reflected from distant stars and planets. Ref. page 124

If you got to this point…then you are doing great! Solving complex phenomena is not an easy task.

Chapters 1, 2, and 3 are the most difficult chapters. But once you get over them….it will be downhill….☺.

So, let your brain continue with 2 and 3 in your discovery journey…

Chapter II

Initial biniverse matter propagation during the auto-chaos entropy, and creation transition phase

What we understand as particles are vibrations or strings of energy fields that pervade all of space. Groups of hydrogen and other new atoms held together by electro-static chemical forces that started exchanging electrons by similar bonding forces as per quantum probabilities of energy state transitions creating new atomic elements during the star formation cycles.

This interesting concept will provide us with clues of how the biniverse propagated with the total amount of atoms known to mankind at the present time. Ref. page 48

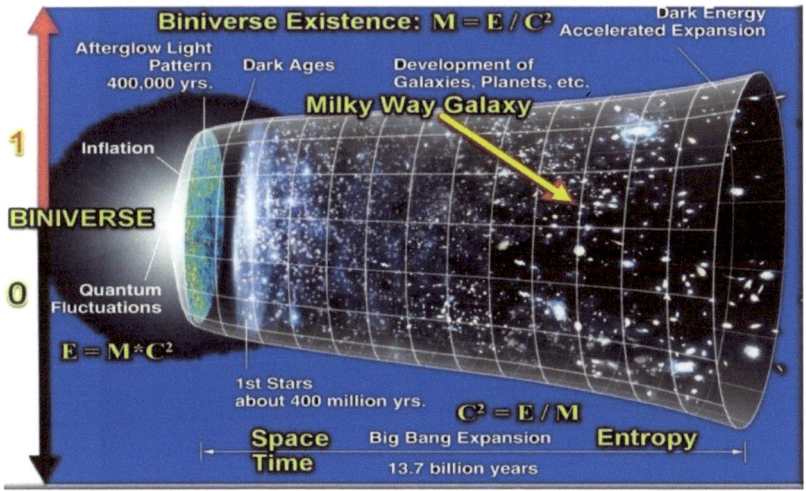

No. 25- Biniverse phase transition expansion

The hydrogen atoms that filled the initial infinite universe 100% started to form nebula clouds from which the stars formed. In these stars, new matter is created at the star's interior nuclear reactions, as trillions of atoms collide frequently inside them for billions of years creating new heavier element particles as per our typical formula of $M = E / C^2$ Ref. Theory of Relativity.

The specific set of reactions thought to be most effective in generating energy in the sun, involves the burning of hydrogen into helium, following the specific sequence of reactions known as the proton-proton reaction. The sun's power of (approximately 386 billion billion megawatts) is produced by well-known nuclear fusion reactions. Each second about 700,000,000 tons of hydrogen atoms are converted into about 695,000,000 tons of helium atoms and 5,000,000 tons (=3.86e33 ergs) of energy in the form of gamma rays among others.

No. 26 - Biniverse galaxies & new matter creation

There are about 10 billion galaxies in the observable biniverse! The number of stars in a galaxy varies, however, estimating an average of 100 billion stars per galaxy also means that there are about approximately 1,000,000,000,000,000,000,000 (1 billion trillion) stars in the observable biniverse! Everyone creating new matter, solar systems, and providing energy to planets like Earth. There are multiple stars for every grain of sand on planet earth creating new matter during particles smashing nuclear reactions presently occurring at all time, as per $E=MC^2$ or $M = E / C^2$ Theory of Relativity.

Now let us considers that this chaotic creation has being going on for more than 13.7 billion years and that only ~5% of the universe is visible. The other ~95% is ~70% unknown dark energy, ~ 25% unknown dark matter, black holes, and anti-matter. (Ref. page 110).

Creation of new raw materials by particle smashing in stars, celestial collisions, explosions, and normal life cycles of stars recycles solar systems at the rate shown builds galaxies that are rich in new raw materials for the formation of numerous planets like our planet Earth as per $M = E / C^2$ formula. Ref. page 113.

No. 27 – The expanding biniverse distribution

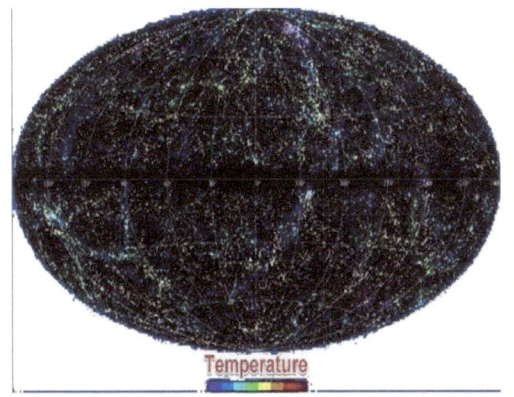

If the figure for all biniverse potentially habitable planets derived by Dr. Frank Drake's well-known equation. Ref. page 50 is correct, or only approximately close to it. Then we could multiply ~20 billion planets by ~500 billion galaxies in the observable universe for an astronomical number of approx. 1,000 trillion Earth-like calculated for possible life habitable planets. *Ref. Kepler +/- telescope* findings.

So out of the initial binary hydrogen atom stars, supernovas, chaotic particle smashing, and celestial collisions. Stars also created black holes' singularities, galaxies, solar systems, planets, moons, comets and asteroids. Now that a completely furnished dynamic chaotic universe has emerged. Let us try to see how the rest of the puzzles fits during the rest of our research trip.

No. 28-The infinite biniverse emerged out of quantum chaos

Chaos and destruction are the integral binary parts of the universal creation. There cannot be life without death, nor death without life. This universal principle applies to even our direct creators, the 10 billion trillion stars of the expanding biniverse.

The Milky Way Galaxy has the sun solar system with 8 planets including our home, Earth. Its size is ~100,000 light years wide across. (light speed is approx. 300,000 Km/sec.)

No. 29 - The Milky Way galaxy

With approximately 100 billion stars. The Milky Way has approximately 200 billion planets. ~8.8 billion stars with Earth-size planets in the habitable temperature zone. A rotation speed of about 670 million miles per hour. An interesting fact is that our Milky Way galaxy is in a collision course with the Andromeda galaxy our nearest galaxy neighbor heading our way for a collision.

But no need to worry, since we will all be dead by that time, and in fact Earth may not even exist by the time they collide with each other. Our Sun will be well out of service before the future chaotic fireworks grand finale.

No. 30. Planets celestial body classification

275 million years equals 1 single Sun's orbit around the Milky Way galaxy.

The requirements for a planet are: Planets must have enough gravity mass so that its own gravity force shapes it into a spherical body. Planets must orbit around a star and not be a satellite of another planet. Ref. *Higgs Boson.*

Sun - Inner Planets:
1. Mercury - Hottest & Coldest / No Rotation
2. Venus – Gas
3. Earth - Water / Solid / Organic life
4. Mars - Solid with some polar ice & liquid water
5. Jupiter- Ongoing storm that looks like big red spot

Earth orbital speed around the Sun is approx. 20 miles/sec.

The Milky Way Galaxy is ~100K light years wide across

No. 31- Milky Way galaxy - *Solar system outer planets:*
6. Saturn - Rings
7. Uranus – Vertically standing **vs.** Ref. other planets
8. Neptune - Gas
9. Pluto / Planet Moon... demoted from planet
   Pluto's Moon - Charon

2003 UB313–Ceres a dwarf planet classified as asteroid.

Summary: **This mystery puzzle is hereby given a possible solution. Ref. Astrophysics, Cosmology, Physics.**

How matter was created out of nothing probability?

The visible Biniverse 5% atomic *matter* emerged from initial 100% quantum hydrogen transition phase due to an unbalanced binary negative and positive energy fields. Then new matter was created by stars, particle smashing in celestial collisions, explosions per *$M=E/C^2$*

The Observer's Reality - Miscellaneous notes

Notes:

The technical reading will be getting much easier now that we have all the raw building materials for our neighborhood. The Milky Way Galaxy (100,000 light years wide). The speed of light is ~186,282 miles/second or 299, 792, 458 m / s) - Ref. Fig. 1a at page 2.

$E=MC^2$ or $M = E / C^2$ and $C = \sqrt{E/M}$

Where: E = Energy   M = Matter   C = Speed of light

Every new chapter will help you see a new piece of the puzzle until you get the whole picture by *The End* at page 137 of this discovery journey, you will uncover all the mysteries that defines our human experience in physical, atomic, and sensory perception of true reality with our bias visual filters and personal modulated perception views. Ref. fig. No. 1 at page 2.

Brain tips: Repeat to remember....There are four stages for our brain to process new information: Input encoding, memory storing, and/or registering, retrieving the information, and forgetting nonessential memories.

Now let us continue our research discovery journey...

Chapter III

Solar systems, Planets, Moons, & the formation of Earth

Earth and the other seven planets in our solar system formed about 4.6 billion years ago in a giant disc-shaped solar nebula. This occurred through collisions of atomically raw materials that also formed the Sun.

Gravity slowly gathered these gaseous clouds and dust together into clumps which became the Sun. The gravity of the sun pulled asteroids and small early planets to rotate around it. In this same way, moons orbits the planets, that orbit the stars, orbiting around the galaxies.

No. 32 – Solar system view

Solar winds swept away lighter elements, such as hydrogen and helium, leaving only heavy rocky material which led to the creation of smaller terrestrial worlds like Earth. The early planet Earth suffered many giant collisions with asteroids and comets. Eventually, earth's gravity captured some of this surrounding material to form the moon.

The moon started orbiting around the larger Earth planet due to the typical gravity attraction force. *Ref. Higgs Boson.*

Stars, supernovas, neutrons, pulsars, and black holes created by cycles of star's deaths, or by hypernovas' explosions, and collisions were a lot more abundant and common during the early universe. Black holes, galaxies, solar systems, and planets were formed in a chaotic initial planetary evolution with all physical and dynamic creative forces.

During billions of years, trillions of diverse galactic planetary formations created new raw sub-atomic particles, and atomic materials were created as per the Periodic Table of Elements. Ref. page 48.

Earth and its composition materials were created by the universe after approximately 9 billion years of chaotic multi-element creation, and an infinite number of celestial particle collisions (like trillions of galaxy-sized particle colliders - Ref. CERN). After the initial biniverse emergence or big-bang, energy inflation of a "Quantum Phase Transition", or the unbalanced binary event that took place. (Ref. Biniverse graph - Page 116).

Presently, there are approximately 118 different elements known to exist on planet Earth, by which everything we know to exist in this planet is made of, including ourselves. Ref. Fig. 37 at page 48.

All the elements where created by the stars. The stars in the universe are the creators of all the elements in the universe by converting hydrogen into helium, oxygen, carbon, nitrogen, phosphorus, sulfur, iron, calcium, magnesium, zinc, potassium, etc. All known elements to humanity at present time were created by trillions of hypernova events during approx. ~13.77 billion years.

No. 33 – Earth's view - Earth's crust is made up of 47% oxygen approx., ~27% silicon, ~8% aluminum, ~5% iron, ~4% calcium, and ~2% of magnesium, potassium, and sodium. It is 46 miles deep and Earth also is approximately 70% covered with oceans, at an averaging of ~2.5 miles deep, and or (~4 Km deep).

Knowing that the composition of water is 2 hydrogen atoms and one oxygen atom (H_2O), we can see how water molecules are created. Keep in mind that the universe is ~95% hydrogen and all the stars like our sun are also created by this same basic hydrogen element.

Our Milky Way galaxy presently has approx. 100 billion of stars doing the typical creation process, and in the whole universe/biniverse there may be a total of approximately 100 trillion stars doing the same thing, even at present time creating new solar systems like ours.

Now let us try to see the rest of the mystery puzzles.

No. 34 – Milky way & Earth location

No. 35 - Earth evolutionary chaotic formation

<u>Summary:</u> This mystery puzzle is hereby given a possible solution. Ref. Astrophysics, Physics, Geology.

How <u>Earth</u> was created out of "matter" probability?

Planet Earth emerged out of the solar system by gravitational forces using biniverse's raw atomic material elements created by stars' trillions life cycles during ~ 13.77 billions of years of planetary universal evolutionary creations as per $M = E / C^2$ formula.

The Observer's Reality - Miscellaneous notes

Notes:

Well, we got to the point where we have our Milky Way galaxy, the solar system, and planet Earth. For the biniverse this was an easy task. *"No rush"* and it does this all the time; this type of creation is just the natural way. The universe does not have any problems with it.

For us humans, it is a different story. Where do you want to start? But that is part of our reality that is very important for us to understand, and accept to agree with the most current scientific knowledge about reality.

Some Reality Facts:

The Earth is approximately 4.543 billion years old. Age found by radioactive dating. Or the ratio between the number of carbon 14 and carbon 12 isotopes. Radioactive decay with time....

Isotopes: Atoms having the same atomic number but different mass numbers.

The world population by the end of 2017 will be approx. 7.50 billion – As per United Nations calculations data.

A new birth in the world takes place every ~8 seconds vs. one death approximately every ~11 seconds,

USA population by the end of 2017 will be approx. 325 million as per United States Census Bureau data.

But now that we are on a 1-2-3 roll, the technical reading will get much easier. Let us keep going, exploring more of the observer's research findings……..☺.

Chapter IV

Creation of minerals, clay, crystals, organic, materials, vegetation, and Earth-life biology.

There are approximately 3,800 known minerals on Earth. However, most of these are rare. Of the 3,800 minerals, only ~200 varieties are most common; like: Gold, silver, iron, nickel, lead, copper, sulfur, zinc, etc.

No. 36-Earth's Natural Minerals - Ref. fig. 37 page 48

Minerals have different atomic structures, and therefore different characteristics that makes them useful for many different applications that take advantage of their unique response to external forces like temperature, pressure, light, voltage, humidity, electric currents, etc.

To a geologist, however, a mineral must have all five of the following characteristics:

1. Must be naturally occurring (not man made) **2.** Must be a solid (not liquid or gas) **3.** Must have a definite chemical composition. **4.** Must be inorganic (not produced exclusively by living organisms or biological processes) and **5.** Must have a crystalline structure (an orderly, internal, repeating arrangement of atoms). Ref. Atomic structure Fig. No. 37

In summary, a mineral is a naturally occurring, inorganic, solid element or compound, with a definite composition and a regular internal crystal structure.

We can observe that there seems to be a universal process, or a natural way in which energy forces seem to be the driving force for all creation, maintenance, changes, and/or evolutionary processes that affects everything in many creative, yet uncontrolled ways.

No. 37 - Periodic Table of Elements

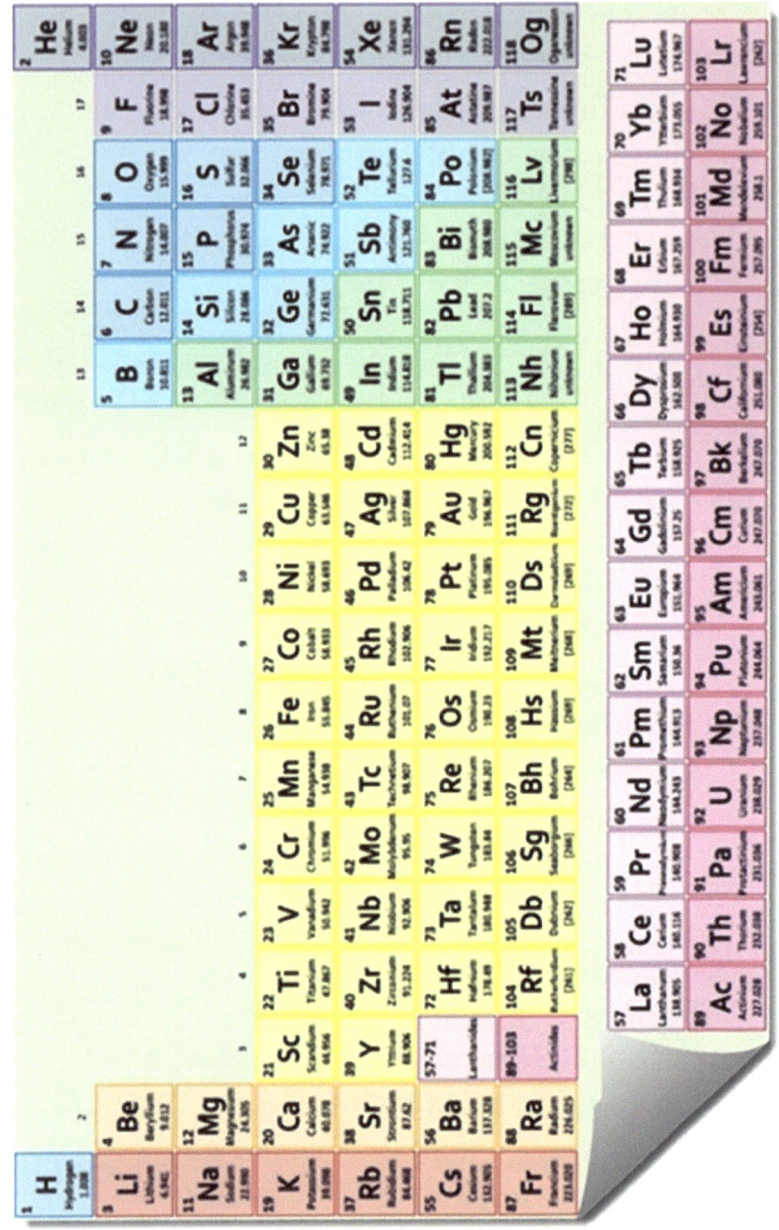

Elements atomic structure

No. 38 – Biniverse dynamic chaotic evolution

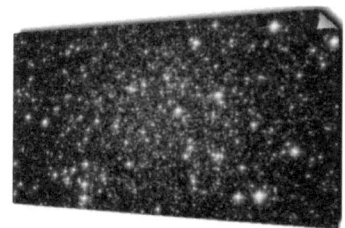

This chaotic universal creation process has been taking place for approximately 13.77 billion years across the infinite space with more than ~10 billion trillion stars spreading all types of materials with collisions, supernova explosions, meteorites, comets, galactic mergers, and black holes gravity attraction forces.

In the natural chaotic way of creation following the law of probabilities in which, "given time everything is possible," all presently existing materials on Earth therefore became available using no more than nature's chaotic creation and time to start performing all kind of evolutionary equivalent experiments in which millions of biochemical reactions using specific combinations of elements (including carbon, hydrogen, nitrogen, and oxygen that combine to form proteins and nucleic acids which eventually can even replicate DNA-RNA genetic code) came about by this natural evolutionary process.

Therefore, the basic components needed for the existence of life are made by natural universal processes.

This process is available everywhere since the formation of the first stars, supernovas, and chaotic celestial collisions also formed billions of new planets.

Estimating the total number of planets in the 10 billion trillion stars of the universe is difficult, but one statistical study suggests that in the Milky Way, each star has an average of 1.6 planets, yielding ~160 billion possible "alien planets" in our Milky Way. Our Sun is only one of the estimated 200 to 400 billion planetary systems with stars that has a planet with the basic components needed for diverse life to exist and thrive.

All the basic elements found on planet Earth were formed in stars and distributed throughout space through numerous giant explosions called supernovas and hypernovas for over ~13.77 billion of years until now.

No. 39–Life in the Milky Way galaxy - Since these essential universal chemicals all are quite common in other places in the biniverse, we can also therefore expect, that the development of life somewhere else is very possible. But also at very far away planets.

Following the *Drake equation formula* for <u>only</u> our own Milky Way galaxy, it states that:

$N = R^{*} \cdot f_p \cdot n_e \cdot f_l \cdot f_i \cdot f_c \cdot L$ Where:

- N = The number of civilizations in the Milky Way galaxy whose electromagnetic emissions are detectable. [At our Sun's solar system location]
- R^{*} = The rate of formation of stars suitable for the development of intelligent life.
- f_p = The fraction of those stars / planetary systems.
- n_e = The number of planets, per solar system, with an environment suitable for life.
- f_l = The fraction of suitable planets on which life appears.
- f_i = The fraction of life bearing planets on which intelligent life emerges.
- f_c = The fraction of civilizations that develop a technology that releases detectable signs of their existence into space.
- L = The length of time such civilizations release detectable signals into space.

Summary:

This calculation yields approximately 160 billion possible "alien planets" with intelligent life in our galaxy alone. We all live in a biological universe where life is just a very common and natural phenomenal biological evolutionary process.

Using Albert Einstein's Theory of Relativity Formula $E=MC^2$ that defines the conversion of energy into matter, and considering that the known universe in which we live is presently ~ 95% hydrogen atoms with only ~5% already converted into visible matter, the potential for life creation, and evolution and its variations is mind blowing and almost infinite limitless for the biniverse.

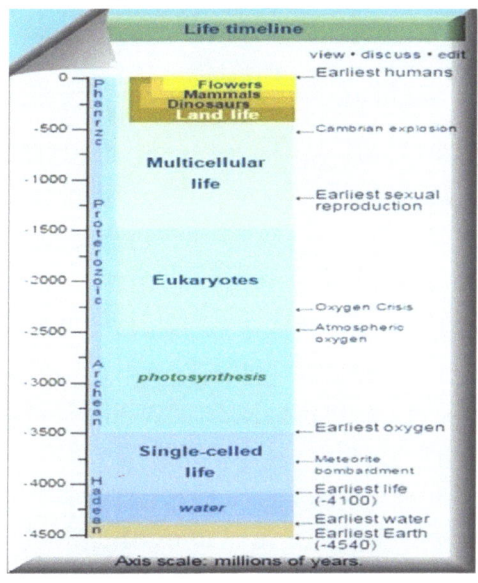

All basic life forms arose spontaneously on Earth simply as an emergent property of inert materials under numerous influences of different energy forces in which nature had the time, and all resources to interact in numerous possible combinations, while trying most typical

No. 40–Earth's life evolution - chaotic natural fractals of evolution algorithms and many highly accidental electro-magnetic chemical reactions were produced by lighting's high voltage, and high electric current strikes.

These strikes of electricity went through all types of atoms, separating, and merging them into new molecules and amino acids. With volcanic high temperature thermals using three basic elemental requirements for life on Earth found in abundance in the form of liquid water, numerous essential chemicals, and different energy sources available just about everywhere on earth, hereby making the bio-chemical emergence of life a new normal, and typical natural reality. See Fig. 120- Page 114.

No. 41 – Initial marine life evolution

~4.5 billion years provided sufficient time to try trillions of messy, drastic and chaotic combinatory possibilities. During this period, clay crystalline chemistry turned into biological simple life forms able to replicate primitive structures. These simple life forms used different types of energies to reproduce in all simple ways. Driven by typical energy efficiency, these evolutionary principles took over following a natural process to improve efficient energy survival of the species. This is still the driving force for evolutionary epigenetic progress going on in all living species today.

Algae was the first living organism on Earth to use chlorophyll, a sun energy converting natural algorithm as a revolutionary natural energy efficiency process.

Chlorophyll is the molecule that absorbs sunlight and uses its energy to synthesize carbohydrates from C_O2 and H_2O or water. This process is known as photosynthesis and is the typical basis for sustaining the life processes of all plants using sun-provided energy.

It was from these initial primitive life forms that gradual evolution took place and numerous more complex biological forms of multiple and different plants eventually developed within the vegetable area.

There are many types of algae like Green Algae, Red & Purple Algae, Yellow & Brown Algae, Blue-Green Algae, Eelgrass, etc.

Characteristics of some types of algae are:
1. It has a nucleus with a proper nuclear membrane.
2. It contains membrane-bound organelles such as endoplasmic reticulum, golgi apparatus, and the special mitochondria that has plastids present.
3. Cell wall has cellulose which are the basic proteins present in DNA. Ref. Fig. 9 -10 & 10a at pages 17 – 18 – 19.

Algae reproduces by all forms of reproduction, that is: a). Vegetative, b). Asexual and c). Sexual forms.

The nucleus has a proper nuclear membrane and sexual reproduction does take place (eukaryotic nature).

The cell lacks basic proteins in its DNA (Prokaryotic nature).

Mesokaryotic algae have both the characteristic features of Prokaryotic and Eukaryotic Algae.

Note: Algae lacks the complex structures of evolved true plants: like roots, stems, and true leaves.

No. 42 – Initial marine vegetation

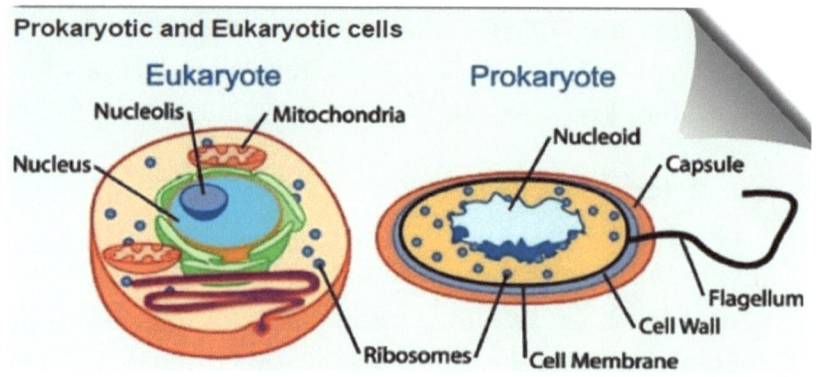

No. 43 - 43a - Initial simple life, single cell organisms

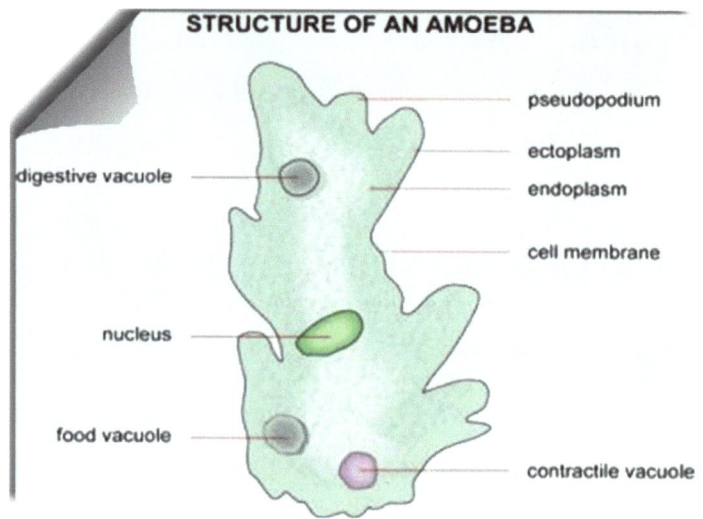

Summary: This mystery puzzle is hereby given a possible solution. Ref. Geology, Biology, Genetics.

How Earth's minerals, and life's biology were created probability.

"Initial simple life forms emerged" out trillions of natural trial and error electro-chemical reaction combinations performed by natural processes around the whole planet for over 4.5 billion of years. Once life's required chemicals became available, life evolved using natural survival of the fittest processes and environmental fractal survival algorithm adaptations.

The Observer's Reality - Miscellaneous notes

No. 44 - Simple lab. life creation experiment

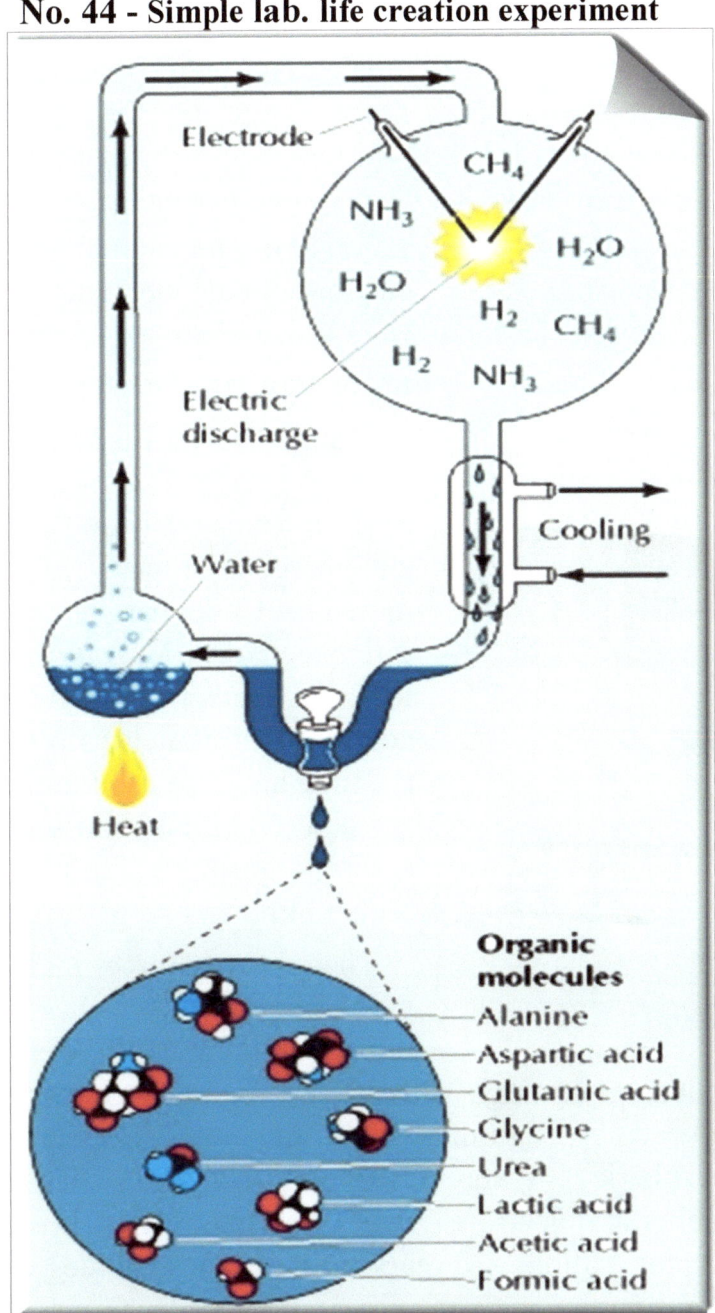

By: Stanley Miller

Chapter V

DNA-RNA based organic life of human's biology

The Last Universal Common Ancestor (LUCA) of all life is the hypothetical, first cell-like structure that was somehow created. It is from this, that original primitive cells evolved into what we now call *biological life*.

The spontaneous formation of organic molecules was first demonstrated experimentally in the lab in the 1950s by Stanley Miller in his lab's life creation experiment.

No. 44a – Lab. simple life creation experiment

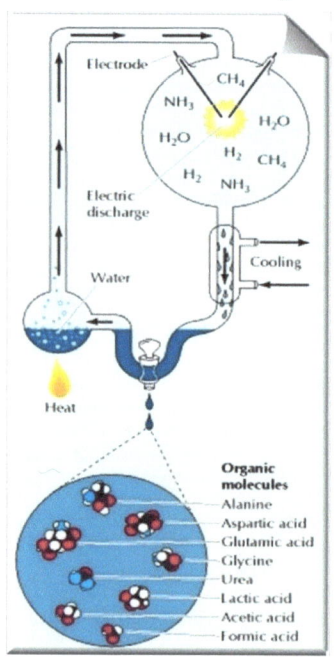

Simple initial *LUCA*, our life ancestors of biology forms arose spontaneously on Earth as an emergent property of inert materials. Under hard numerous influences of all energy forces, these materials interacted under conditions in which nature had the time and resources to try all possible recombination's using natural algorithms like fractals, with all known energy forces.

These energy forces included gravity, nuclear, the sun's weak radiation along with chemical reactions under high voltage, and high electric currents produced by lighting, high and low temperatures, atmospheric pressures, and multi-millions of other combinatory electromagnetic experiments took place on earth for billions of years. Due to these forces, very crude, fragile, and primitive simple life forms were created through this crude chaotic evolutionary process.

Eventually, the initial primitive simple life forms that populated the planet for more than 3.5 billion of years, evolved into more efficient life forms always driven by energy most efficiency conversion usage. *Allowing a transition from the basic inert material elements to new crude, fragile, primitive simple forms of algae, fungi, and more complex bacterial life formed by using evolution's natural algorithms, and fractal systems.*

The LUCA process is not unique to planet Earth. The process of life creation is so chaotic and random that given enough time and resources the combinatory experiments are a natural occurrence. In fact, no two snowflakes, no animals, no humans, no planets are ever created 100% identical. *Everything in the universe is unique. Similar but never identical due to entropy. RAZ*

Change is the only universal constant. Entropy is a natural law of creation through its chaotic process. Therefore, a balanced binary original system in which $0 = +1$, or a quantum transition is a natural probability or possibility that automatically triggers quantum energy changes as an emergence of unbalance state of the universe that occurs in a phenomenal universal natural process across trillions of galaxies as part of a chaotic and natural creation force. This is the reason why it is so difficult for us to comprehend when we try to find a beginning for existence of energy. *It just always was.*

In other words, initially space-time did not yet exist.

The unbalance of original binary state from zero to one (**0** to **1**) was the catalyst, or quantum transition phase or point at which space-time was created. At the quantum "Bang" moment the space in the universe became 100% full of simple binary hydrogen atoms as an (- & +) emergence phenomenon. Ref. Page 116 Binary Graph Theory

Remember when we were told that energy cannot be created or destroyed, that it was always just there. Well, the binary hydrogen energy balanced universe emerged out of a positive and negative (- & +) energy field we call "nothing." These were the only two natural probabilities: existence & non-existence from binary radiation energy.

Both with the same mathematical and physical values. Eventually, energy created mass at the speed of creation expansion squared or the speed of light 300,000 km/sec. as per $M=E/C^2$ Ref. Albert Einstein Theory of Relativity.

This is the conventionally accepted scientific formula for the conversion of energy into matter at present time.

Note: Which *"Nothing Table"* is possible in reality

$0 = No\ Energy$	No Space	No Time	No
$1 = Energy$	Space	No Time	No
Binary Energy	Space	Time	Yes

No. 45 – Binary Table 1 - Energy – Space -Time

A radical new idea is that we need to reassess the definition of the term *nothing*. *Nothing* literally has a language definition, but physically the way we presently perceive it is wrong. *In the physical universe, nothing* cannot exist. Entropy makes it impossible to reverse the arrow of time after creation, and not a thing, *nothing* is an impossibility.

Nothing is just another of man's illusions. Energy is everywhere, it cannot be created or destroyed. Energy always existed, and was just there in the universe that emerged from unbalanced binary energy field of (0 to 1).

Then along came evolutionary chaos, the natural sculpturing tool using energy, efficiency, natural selection, and survival of the fittest as the natural evolutionary creation algorithms used for life's fuel.

No. 46-Human cell – The next two chapters are the most interesting of this book. They will cover life! Our life as human beings from these 6-different point of views: **1.** How we were created, **2.** What we are, **3.** The illusion of our reality and perceptions, **4.** Reasons why we are here, **5.** Do we have free will? And **6.** Human spirituality, or personal religious needs of human beings compared to present correlations, and other spiritual religious teachings of metaphysics, and/or scientific modern new concepts.

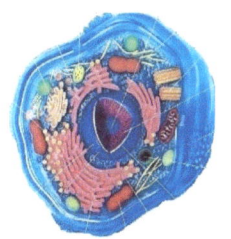

1. How humans were created:

The first biological cells appeared on Earth about ~3.5 billion years ago, approximately 1 billion years after the Earth was initially formed. It has taken an additional ~3.5 billion of the natural evolution process for us to be here on Earth as human beings at present time.

2. We are biological human organic cells that are made of basic chemical compositions of approximately 65% Hydrogen, ~18% Carbon, ~3% Nitrogen, ~1% Phosphorus, and ~ 13% trace elements like Sulfur, Iron, and Calcium. With ~ 200 bones skeleton, and ~100 trillion of cells and bacteria.

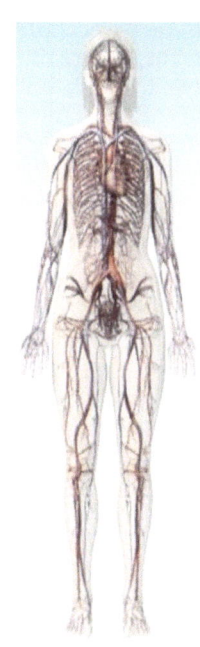

No. 47 – Human Body

No. 48 – Homo Sapiens - *Man // Evolution Ref. Info.*

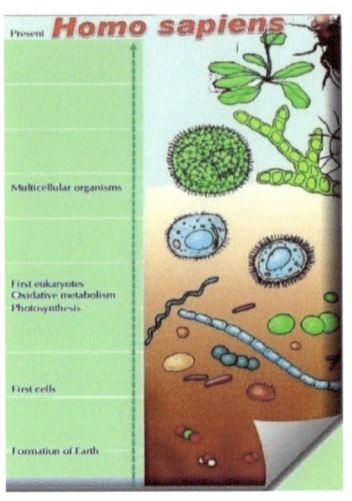

2a. Using typical chemistry scientific knowledge to study the composition of matter, and energy, the following is a summary and very compacted description of human beings' life organic cell structure of its components: Life = Energy = Atoms = ~118 Elements = Matter = Carbon & Hydrogen. (See Fig. 123 at Page 118).

No. 49 - Life Evolution - Humans basic 2 molecules are: Carbon & Hydrogen = H_2O = 2H + 1 Oxygen = Water, Organic molecules = Particles = 20L mirror amino acids = ~ 5 Categories of Proteins = Amino acids long chains chromosomes = DNA + RNA = Genes = 46 chromosomes per cell = x2 chains linked 100 to 500 amino acids protein molecules. *Glad you are still with me.*

In addition: Female = X and Male = X or Y. Where XX = Female or if: X+Y = Male with ~3 Billion pairs of nucleotides = Enzymes = Stem cells = Organic cells = Multi-cellular organs = Brain, Heart, Liver, etc. Living organisms = Biological biochemical carbon-based Life = Human beings. *We are very complex organisms.*

The genetic code letters in the double-helix DNA with ~3 billion programmed cells for the human beings = ~ 20,000 genes = ~ 100 trillion cells = reproduction = human evolution process by: X & Y inherited chromosomes = 1 set of 23 from each parent [mother = x23 XX & father x23 X or Y] XY = male baby boy with (testosterone hormones). XX = female baby girl with (estrogen hormones). Easy? Or simply clear as mud? Yes, life is extremely complex for a single page…. ☺.

No. 50 - Chromosomes - 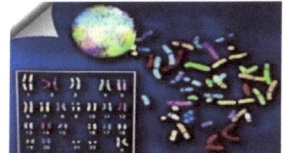 **2b.** The most typical or normal biogenetic cellular organic human life auto reproduction manufacturing is done by evolution that is billions of years old using the chromosomes long strands of double helix DNA chemical amino acid based pairs chains of A<>T & C<>G's individual unique molecular genetic code.

We are one hundred million DNA-based pairs of chromosomes: ~6 billion based-pairs per each of our trillion body cells in human beings, partitioned into ~ 20,000 different genes using a unique blueprint of nanotechnology pre-programmed proteins with Mfg. instructions for ~ 20 different L amino acids chemical units to make ~5 different protein's categories that are ~ 0.1% different for each individual person, never =100%

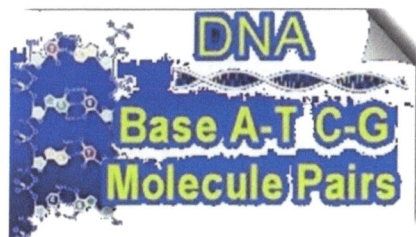 Human cell proteins' specific functions are controlled by turning on or off specific genes in the respective DNA – RNA transcription factors used

No. 51– DNA - to control human's approximately 35 different blood types, antigens, and special multi-functional cell proteins that give us our distinctiveness.

Proteins are what give us our unique physical characteristics and the reason why related specimens share resemblances. Since the + or - tolerance is only ~0.1% plus temporary typical daily numerous mutations of ~ 16,000 per day with only ~ 80% correction factor.

The other 20% of mutations are carry-on, and accumulated in the genetic DNA during all our lives.

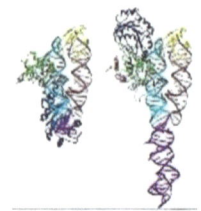
Personal individual proteins control the neuron cells involved in learning, memory, mood, behavior, desires, and perception for the five sensory input filters, and decoding of our life's brain

No. 52 – 3D Proteins - electro-chemical interface of our realities as its perceived by our brains with reference to stored database memory of our life's present and past experiences. These brain memories are recalled by neurotransmitters ion molecules controlled by electro-chemicals impulses traveling at approximately 250 MPH in our ~3 pounds ~15 watts, 100 billion neurons of the brain neuro cells.   **No. 53 – DNA – RNA Molecules**

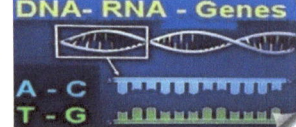

2c. What are human beings? Human beings are made up of approximately ~20K to ~25K genes that are genetically electro-chemical, biological self-programming, self-reproducing, self-repairing, self-learning, and self-auto-evolutionary. In other words, we are fleshy wet sentient robots, multi-cellular intelligence electro-chemical programmable biological auto-genetic living organisms created by an evolutionary process.

We can transfer billions of years of genetic biological information into the next generation for the benefit and survival of our own future human species.

Note: *Cancer cells* are stronger, smarter, evolved, and mutated to prevent their natural death. Also, able to metastases reproduction without normal cellular control trying to be immortal in their quest for their survival against carcinogens, or some chemical agents. This adaptive reproduction is part of their natural defense by using the blood supply to migrate across the body to other organs in case the original tumor is killed and or removed from the host body during cancer treatment or chemotherapy. Ref. page 20.

No. 54 – Human Chromosomes

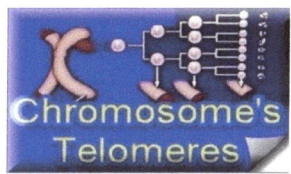

Life's biological cellular design is tough because of its creative complexity which is extremely recursive, adaptive and very responsive to the environmental changes. Its evolution capacity is revolutionarily smart and inventive with options to be genetically programmable, and re-programmable, changing its critical characteristics on as required-basis. Also, human chromosomes can pass the updated genetic code information to the next generations of species to improve their chances of survival in the chaotic world's hostile environments we need to live in.

2d. Humans are formed out of approximately 100 trillion cells using close to 6 feet long DNA double helix chromosomes with approximately ~3 billion bases containing the blue print in approx. 25,000 different genes attached by 4 different molecules described as:
A◇T – C◇G with self-replicating, and repair capability.

The DNA uses a genetic digital code used to express life's required instructions in RNA to manufacture specialized protein molecules using enzymes, and amino acids and/or the biological material for the proper cell functions in the different body multi-organs.

This is an oversimplification of our human body.
(**2e.** What we are), without getting into deep specifics.

<u>Summary:</u> **This mystery puzzle is hereby given a possible solution. Ref. Biology, Genetics, Cell evolution.**

How DNA based human life was created probability.

Human being animals' DNA/RNA-based organic life was created by a natural evolutionary process over approximately 4.5 billion of years in planet Earth where evolution created life's intelligent sophisticated designs.

The Observer's Reality - Miscellaneous notes

Notes:

A) Mother nature's capacity to use fractals and energy efficiency natural algorithms with the natural laws to create intelligent designs cannot be under estimated.

B) The universe, biniverse, and/or multi-verses are equivalent cosmology evolution designs just like human beings are.

C) Mother nature, evolution, and intelligent design are also equivalents design processes similar to each other.

D) All the above can be implemented with, and emerged out of a simple "binary" controlled process. As per the author's graphically described:

Biniverse Binary Theory *Graph: Energy, Space-Time Ref.* Fig. No. 121 - Page 116 - Pages: 57 & 119 Notes...

We are almost halfway, and the most interesting chapters about our reality are coming next.... Hang in there.... Let us continue with our discovery journey inside the observer's brain for this interesting research trip of his new radical paradigm to human's reality.

Human brain reality facts:

Leeches have 32 brains, octopus have 9 brains, jelly fish has none. But humans also have multiple brains contrary to what most people think, that we only have one, including a good friend of mine that lives in Tampa, Fl. ☺

During our evolution, the other brains listed here were added to the original. 1st: lizard or nervous system brain. 2nd: Cerebellum, for motor memory control. 3rd: Emotional limbic system, 4th: Cerebral cortex lobes. The latest addition to the human brain is the frontal lobe.

Ready for a new *"paradox"* ?...Here we go......

Chapter VI

3. The temporary illusion of existence & its end.

Universal life is a biniversal emergent process.... where the biniverse becomes aware of its own existence, and finally can say *I am*, I am you, and you are me. I know now that I do exist throughout the life that I have created by the default laws of the evolutionary chaotic natural process. We are part of it, and were created by the similar atomic material that the universe is made of.

No. 55 – Microscope

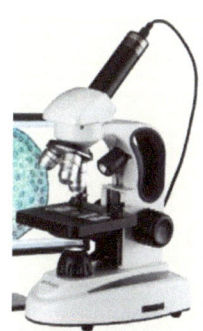

We are the sum total of all our life's experiences. Including the origin of basic life forms with upbringings, and resulting in the very personal mindset of unique personalities that are constantly being reprogrammed by our perceptions of our own unique reality, personal knowledge, all our memories, the education, and environmental influences of our cultural and dynamic life interfaces.

This makes us who we are, and determines how much we can grow, and evolve into even better and more complex physical species. If we look at our genetic composition, we - **No.56– Telescope** can see that we encompass the elements of all the different kingdoms of nature. All biological life on earth including us, depend on each, and every single one of these diverse nature kingdoms for our very evolutionary survival of the present, and future species.

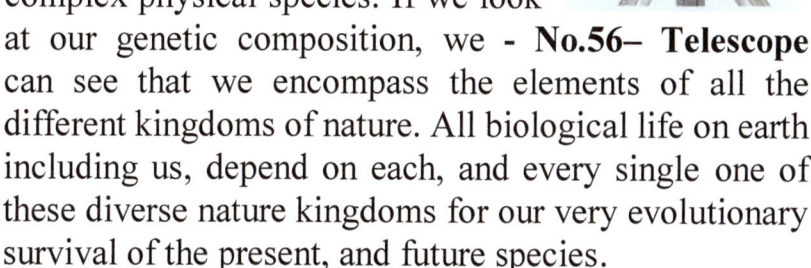

4. Why did we end up in this planet? If we are a result of the Universe's living biological material being aware of its own existence by using our biological sensory perceptions, then we become the observers the universe created, and is experiencing the virtual reality of its own existence using different types of life forms.

Without these different types of biological sensors or observers to detect cause & effect the universe will be a space full of energy fields that are useless, invisible, odorless, tasteless, soundless, and without the sense of touch, and feel of its existence. Then "nothingness" will be the true useless empty nonexistence -X phase reality.

4a. Therefore, we are part of the "Q" universe's requirement for existence. We must be here for it to experience its own existence. I ask you: What is the use to building an infinite universe to keep it empty and devoid of life for eternity? None. Therefore, the **Y** phase.

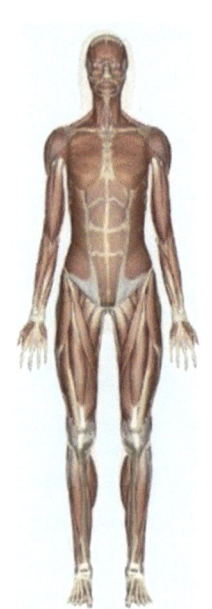

At this point it is important to mention the limitations that are part of all the biological life "Q" sensory awareness, particularly for us human beings.

It is important for humans to improve our perception of the reality that we are experiencing, trying to overcome our sensory limitations. We need to evolve to an even more intelligent higher state.

High enough to develop technological tools to amplify our senses. The use of the most advanced technology will help us overcome the epic illusionary and/or the limitations of our quantum reality, and

No. 57–The observer's human body- "Q" sensory perceptions of our own existence to see the true reality.

5. Do we have free will? Maybe we don't. But exceptional claims also require exceptional evidence of such claims. Well... Only 5% of our decisions are caused by our conscious attention to present situations that we are actually aware of them.

No. 58 – Technology Tools

The other 95% are because of natural embedded genetically preprogrammed solutions all controlled by brain subconscious auto-electro-bio-chemical natural algorithms that keep us alive. Some scientific evidence shows that human's body behavior is controlled by neurobiology, and *100% free will may not exist.* It seems that we only can become aware after the fact. Our awareness is *time lagging* our subconscious thoughts.

Free will is the ability for us to think, choose, or act with *awareness* of our actions. To believe that human beings can be the authors of their own actions, then we need to reject the fact that human actions are determined by biologically controlled organic functions working in automatic mode, and controlling all of our body's cells.

Epigenetics show that we are under programmable genetic methylation control, and that our genes can be switched on or off without our conscious awareness, and with our sensory system out of the loop during this process before, and after we are born. The free will we have over our existence may be the same control we have over our deaths; or not much. It seems that *life* is what happens to us while we were making other plans......

Summary: *This mystery puzzle is hereby given a possible solution. Ref. Biology, Genetics, Neuroscience*

How is our temporary illusion of existence & its end?

Our temporary illusion of existence & its end is determined by genetically programmed natural deaths.

Misc. notes: 3 History correlations. For ref. only.

No. 59 – A – B - C - Dependency needs. The scientific

enlightenment approx. ~ 1,872 years AD or science understanding of the universe…it does agree with B & C below. *No issues*….

1. $E=MC^2$ $M = E/C^2$ or $C = \sqrt{E/M}$ (Theory of Relativity)
2. Energy is everywhere, always existed. It cannot be destroyed. Everything was, or is created by energy.
3. We are made from energy, and are also impermanent.

Christ: Approx. ~ 450 years after Buddha
1. Holy Trinity Mystery (Blind faith)
2. Father + Son + Holy Spirit - ($E = M C^2$)
3. God creator of everything. Always existed, is everywhere, we are created to his image, likeness, and similarities. *Some of 12 Commandments:* 6. Thou shalt not kill – 7. Thou shalt not commit adultery. – 8. Thou shalt not steal – 9. Thou shalt not bear false witness 10. Thou shalt not covet. Etc.
Christian timeline history: Moses ~1,527 - ~1,407 BC
Ten Commandments: ~ 1,487 BC [The Torah books]
Buddha: ~ 1, 000 years <u>after</u> Moses's Torah books…

Gautama Buddha "One who is awake" born in Nepal ~2,500 years ago. Attained enlightenment meditating under a Ficus (bodhi tree) He did not claim to be a God or a Prophet. A teacher of his life philosophies of noble truths with mindfulness meditation

1. Impermanence – Nothing last forever in the universe.
2 Bodiless - Everything changes
3 Everything is Inter-Related-Law of Cause & Effect
The five precepts: 1. No killing, 2. No stealing, 3. No sexual misconduct, 4. No lying, 5. No intoxicants.

We're the observers. *God is everywhere.* **Ref. page 98, 128.**

Chapter VII

6. *The need of our spiritual life experiences*

Infinity is the natural default state of existence and dual binary nonexistence, in the limitless time-space compendium. The original balanced binary energy field was always there. There was no beginning and there is no end. Living and dying is a natural process within this quantum binary field. Ref. Author's Binary Graph page 116.

By default, existence and nonexistence are the two possibilities of the binary phenomenon of emergent infinity. In addition, we must acknowledge that there is no separate-self.

It is impossible to be detached from our creator that made us into its image and/or likeness out of - **No. 59-D – Dependency Needs** the same energy and material in our present biological living human organic forms.

Once we understand the principle of existence and nonexistence, and the fact that separate-self from the universe cannot exist, then we can see the point for our **No. 60 – Galaxy –** existence as main participants of the creation, and evolution. This is one of the reason for our existence. The human need for all answers through spirituality allows an entangled or separate-self mind to freely connect to the source of universal intelligence.

The source of our creation. The universal energy that controls our very human existence, and experiencing of a spiritual virtual awareness as a form of a divine enlightenment perception of our interconnected minds.

 After ~4.5 billion years, the atomic structures were finally made into very complex bio-organic living organisms intelligent enough to be able to ask or **No. 61–Family** - understand its own complex organic living biology. We also became intelligent enough to be aware that we are the result of an *evolutionary chaotic process of the biniverse* by which the universe becomes aware of its own existence. We are part of the universe; created by it, from its own similar atomic structure, elements, matter, and energy likeness. This is our reality.

The spiritual holistic thoughts: **No. 62 – Spirituality**

So, when we think of spirituality in the context of the chaotic entropy of biniverse diversity, we can see ourselves as divine human beings with free will to forget at times who we are. But the fact that we are quantum-entangled with the universe will always remind us of our true nature. We are here as the observers, and being observed by  the universe through our lives, but we'll do a better job if we are present without judgment, and have acceptance to our existence (*as is*) to prevent mental, emotional, and or physical suffering due to non-acceptance of *"reality"*.

No. 63 – Reality = (E=MC² + Law of Cause & Effect)

 If we dare to ignore our *big egos,* and see our creation as an indirect cause of the universe's chaotic evolution, then we may be able to find answers to some of the most profound, and mysterious questions, myths and legends that we have been trying to find answers to as intelligent human beings already for quite some time.

See if you find religious, spiritual, and/or existing scientific correlations to the following statements:

i. The universe was always there…it does not have a beginning nor it does have an end. (Mystery) + (Faith).
ii. The universe is everywhere. It always existed. It cannot be created; nor can it be destroyed. - (Puzzles).
iii. We are made of the same atomic elemental structures, energy, matter and likeness as the same divine creator.
iv. The mystery of the Trinity: Energy = Matter x Universal Speed of expansion squared or $E = M * C^2$
v. To be born, grow, reproduce, and die are natural laws for human beings; as well as to be controlled by genetic natural evolution of the human species.
vi. We are stardust, and shall become stardust after our deaths. Nothing more, nothing less. – Genesis 3:19

Note: There is nothing wrong with having diversity of religious needs to satisfy our own individual search for answers, or having other radical perceptions of reality if we respect, and do not cause harm to each other as spiritual human beings, this is okay. Entropy, diversity, change, chaos, new creations, and acceptance are universal laws for happy co-existence. ☺ *Life is short.*

 =>

No. 64 – Chaos   No. 65 Chaos **Theory** + **Life**

Summary: *This mystery puzzle is hereby given a possible solution. Ref. Theology, Neuroscience, Chaos*

How are our needs for the spiritual life's experience?

The spiritual experiences during our lives are human needs in the search for answers to our reality.

The Observer's Reality - Miscellaneous notes

Notes: I am glad that you are still with me....
Divinity & Spirituality - Ref. page 128.

5. Do we have free will?   Ref. Top of page 67

I will like to clarify now that the answer is a binary ambiguous yes, and no (a contradiction). Since our brains perception have an actual time delay between our neuron's firing to signal a command action after the voltage threshold is exceeded vs. our actual cell's response time and awareness; This delay can easily be seen during involuntary reflexes movements that in some cases can even cause injuries. But we become aware only after our cells act in the auto-reflex action.

In other words, we can become aware after the fact, and then we choose to agree with our thoughts, and may not even agree with them after some careful analyzes takes place. Presently there are some ongoing brain studies on this subject in Germany and the USA. But remember to keep an open mind....Sorry. but some times reality is not what it seems to be, *and that is a fact.*

Note: Depending on the speed of the observation and or measurement both "binary" options can be true.

This old philosophical human free will debate is very interesting, and worthy of additional research online.

Free will proverbial paradox question. Ref. Page 67

It is with our brains that we are going to find the answers, and put this whole puzzle together. I left the brain for the last chapters.... typical to leave the best for last. It gets very interesting in these last chapters....

Let us get more pieces of the puzzle. Dig in....and enjoy the reading.

Chapter VIII

The human physical brain and the virtual 4-D mind sensory illusions

No. 66 – Neuron

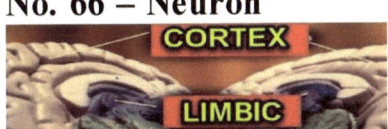

No. 67 - The Human Brain - The driving force for the evolution of life on planet Earth has been the natural selection of the species. This ensures their survival and reproductive chances to pass on an improved organic and genetic information to the next generations with updated mutations that will be kept, if they are found beneficial.

At present time, the human brain is evolving trying to keep us alive. The frontal lobe is the part of the brain undergoing more changes to help us survive. It is the decision-making controller, and we need to be aware that there are some false illusions of our reality, and some misconceptions in the perceptions of this reality.

No. 68 - Human Brain

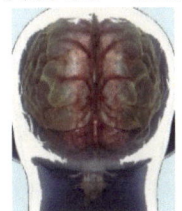

An example is that most people when asked what do they love with…will answer that they love with their hearts. The heart is just a blood pumping muscle.

We love with our *limbic system.* Our perceptions of love, feelings, and emotions are electro-chemical stimuli to our brain neuron cells in the form of molecular ion neurotransmitters, with respective synapses receptors decoding such information regarding previous memory knowledge, past and present emotional associations.
Ref. page 24. Love is a "chemical reaction" …. ☺

Most people also think that they find most food taste in their tongues instead of the olfactory system which controls most of our taste sense stimuli.

In addition, we are normally not aware that white is just the combination of all colors being reflected to our eyes.

We are limited by our senses to be able to see the reality of our world as it is, instead of a modulated one.

A red object is anything but -**No. 69 – Brain Neuron** red…red being the electromagnetic wavelength that it does not absorb and therefore is reflected. All sounds must be intelligently decoded within the brain, since sounds are only just modulated atmospheric pressure changes. Colors are only different electromagnetic frequencies decoded by the observer's misperceptions of true reality being decoded within our brains. Unreal….?

The human brain organ is ~3 pounds, ~100 billion neurons, and ~1 trillion neuron cell connections. It runs hot, with ~3% body mass, using ~20% of body's energy.

Contrary to popular legend we use our whole brain 100% of the time. But just <u>not all parts</u> of it at once.

Is the human brain a living mini-universe? The human brain is the most complex "object" known in the universe/biniverse.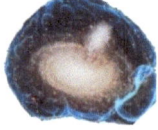

There seems to be a very -*No. 70–"Q" Mini-universe* strange but beautiful comparison between the human brain and the known "Q" atomic biniverse/universe.

Now I am not the only one proposing a connection between the structure of the universe and the structure of the human brain. If we compared our brain neurons to the universe, we will find that they structurally do look strangely, and peculiarly or coincidentally very similar.

As per the following brain information below shows:

The human brain has ~100 billion neuron cells capable of making interconnections. Each neuron has a "bandwidth" of 1,000 cells. Therefore, the brain can have ~1 million billion synaptic connections, yielding a total of 10x 1 million zeros. This is in comparison to (10x only (79 zeros) that equals approximately all particles in the known visible and materialized present "Q" atomic visible universe created as per the $M = E / C^2$ formula.

No. 71 – Brain Neuron's Mapping

The brain ionic neurotransmitter's electro-chemical signals travel through the neuron forest to form the basis of our memories, thoughts, emotions, feelings, real and virtual consciousness, with all our awareness of being. Ref. https://www.youtube.com - Brain videos searches

Electro-chemical signal stimuli give us the inner mental capability to be aware and able to experience our own existence within the actual multidimensional space & time physical paradigm. This use of all our sensory perceptions of the external world, and stimuli inputs as the present world is detected, or interpreted by our brains at each present dynamic moment of our lives allows our brains to decode our present human reality as detected by our human's limited "Q" sensory perceptive systems.

Human brain and evolution. In order to adapt, and survive we have about 9 different intelligence capacities:

1. Logical = math + science
2. Spatial = space + visual
3. Verbal = memory + languages
4. Social = interpersonal + social networking
5. Motor = musical + physical sports skills
6. Kinesthetic = energy use + muscles + nerves
7. System 1 & system 2 type of
Memory skills = inputs /outputs autonomy + competence + interests + connections with confirmation bias + novelty + experiences + creativity + mastering new challenges
8. Emotional = intellectual + memory learning and recall capacity **No. 72 – The "Q" Brain**
9. Subconscious = genetic + imagination + creativity + autonomous survival control systems.

The above evolutionary conceptualization of our mental skills, and the brain capacity for integration using existing acquired knowledge, allows us to use normal human brain intuition, reason, logic, or use of our experiences, and feelings to develop superior insight for analysis capability, and/or just above-average intuitive mental capacity to solve problems for our own required survival to be able to pass-on our genes to the next generation to help ensure their own survival chances.

No. 73 – The "Q" brain problem solver

Allow your brain to decode following encrypted words:
Tde br2in h3s d cap4c17y 2 f?nd or d?c?de m1s?ing info., & f?nd sol?=?ns by int=G>ing ex1t3ing m???mores, & kno@#$dge i=to d req=?^ed unk???n sol=?t=ons. I re!!ly d 1iqe d obs1#3er met987ys1cs bkok a 1()t s0 fr. *(See page 136 for solution).*

The normal functioning of the physical brain activity across trillions of electrochemical connections and transmission of ion neurotransmitters, creates a virtual connection with the surrounding part of the universe around us to allow us to perceive reality in our minds.

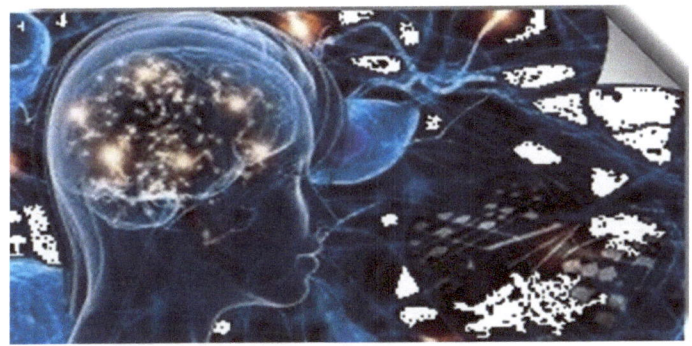

No. 74 – The virtual 4-D mind

The virtual mind is an electrochemical energy field that acts as a control center for our behavior in the physical world. It allows us to thrive and interact with outside environmental stimuli with guidance from previously acquired DB. memories, while using present sensory inputs from our close environment surroundings.

Due to this epigenetic interface with the inside, and outside environment, all our genetic composition is reprogrammed to adapt using feelings, and emotions as a biofeedback loop that self-calibrates to generate the proper response to the stimuli received while also making use of our related memories, and knowledge previously acquired to help us survive, thrive and evolve.

Consciousness is the inner mental capability to be aware. It also allows us to be able to experience our own existence within the actual 4-Dimensional space/time physical paradigm. The use of all our brain sensory perceptions of the external world is interpreted by our brain activity and stimulated neurons that create our minds and reality awareness. But with time delays factor.

This perception of reality can be turned off and on, amplified, attenuated, distorted, changed, shifted, and/or changed. These changes in perceptions can occur before or after the fact, using technological electro-chemical stimuli to the neuron cells in the brain. Since the actual interpretation is based on interaction of ~100 billion neuron cells dynamically doing an active speedy and a very dynamic multi-comparative memory recreation using electro-chemicals stimuli in

No. 75– Mind - neurotransmitters across a virtual mind network of neuron cells to create our "Q" present reality.

No. 77 - The physical brain, and the virtual 4-D mind

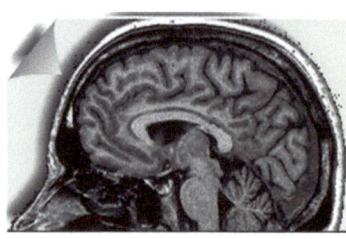 

No. 76- Consciousness

<u>Summary:</u> This mystery puzzle is hereby given a possible solution. Ref. Neuroscience, Genetics, Organic cell biology.

How our physical brain creates our mind's 4-D reality?

The physical brain creates our mind's reality with sensory physical stimuli perceptions of our biological senses.

The Observer's Reality - Miscellaneous notes

Notes:

Congratulations! You are past the 8 most difficult chapters for solving the whole puzzle! It is downhill from here on during this discovery research trip. Now you will see how all pieces of the puzzle fall into their places......

A very interesting and important neuroscientific fact about the brain is its *neuroplasticity*. The ability it has to dynamically change as required in real time and on a daily basis.

Remember in the earlier pages about *brain priming* at the preliminary sections of the book, from here to the time you get to the last page 137, this book is taking advantage of your brain's *neuroplasticity* as you undertake this discovery journey of new subjective paradoxical topics that will redefine how you will see reality after you finish reading this book, and see existence from different metaphysical points of view.

You are now part of some of the world's greatest thinkers that have attempted to find the answers to the myriad of mysteries about our human physical reality.

After you finish this book, you will be prepared to *come to your very own conclusions* on the subjects covered hereby hopefully with an open informed mind.

But now let us keep going...more research to do....

Chapter IX

The philosophical existence illusion of our reality

Philosophy as defined by any modern dictionary is the human love of wisdom by pursuit of intellectual means and moral self-discipline. The investigation of causes, effects, and laws that underlie reality. A system of philosophical inquiry or physical demonstrations.

These research inquiries into the nature of things are based on some logical reasoning rather than empirical methods. Also, the critique and analysis of fundamental beliefs as they come to be conceptualized and/or formulated during the synthesis of all old, and new intellectual human learning of the world around us. But also, philosophy covers the study of everything already found in the universe which requires an intellectually clever explanation of it.   **No. 78 – Illusions vs. Reality**

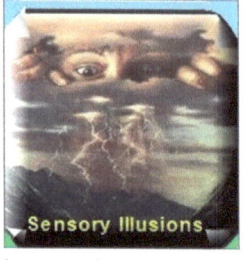

Metaphysics is the radical branch of philosophy that deals with first principles and seeks to explain the nature of being or reality (ontology), and of the origin and/or structure of the universe (cosmology). It is also closely associated with the study of the real nature of human knowledge (epistemology).

Keep in mind that metaphysics is also a speculative philosophy by which we can try tackle most popular unknowns, phenomena, and all mysteries in subtle ways.

Metaphysics is used for difficult reasoning that seeks to explain the nature of being or the true scientific emergence of our Q. reality in the universe while dealing with *natural mysterious unknowns* and/or unexplainable mythologies, legends, and/or unknown "Q" phenomena.

Metaphysics also allows us to use new concepts based on speculative science and/or abstract reasoning characterized by an intellectual challenging of present scientific concepts, and/or new philosophical schools of thought that differ from conservative ways of thinking for a more liberal approach to the chaotic creative way in which universal evolution seems to work by which change seems to be the only real biniversal constant.

Nothing is static, everything is different. This is our real reality. Trying to stay in the past is not progress, and is not conductive to our long-term survival as human species.

This is also the branch of philosophy that deals with the first principle of things, including abstract concepts such as being, knowing, substance, cause and effect, identity, existence of all Q. energies in space–time modern paradigm.

Metaphysics is also the philosophical science that examines the nature of true reality, including the relationship between mind and matter, substance and attribute, fact and value, and is the tool used for the writing of this informative book to try to find answers to our actual human true reality.

No. 79- The Mind

Our humanity: The human brain is the most complex organ in the universe. It has evolved to be able to question its creation. In addition, after also being aware of the complexity of the universe, it is also interested to 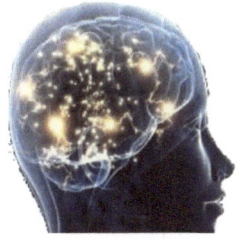 know all the direct mystical/physical relationship of its own existence, and all the binary evolutionary creations.

One way of acquiring answers to these questions is by the acquisition of modern intellectual knowledge in all possible scientific fields available to us new human Homo Sapiens during our evolutionary present age of the newly created modern advanced and interconnected online civilization.

In a new knowledge and technical skill innovation-driven world, the survival of the fittest is now decided instead of by brute force as before; nowadays is mostly by our intelligent savvy capacity, the high education, inventiveness, expertise, and/or new computers with artificial intelligence tools. Also by the powers of new international networks that influence stimulates our sociotechnical global economic environments of the new globally interconnected economic multi-communities.

No. 80 –Auto-Blood Cell Analyzer Technology

This use of tools that allows to engage in symbiotic skilled relationships with experts in different technical fields nowadays play a survivability very important role given our human genetic limitation in perception, and cognition allowing us to increase our intelligence to be able to learn new ways to adapt, and to survive in a changing brave new technologically, economic-driven chaotically changing, beautiful, but dangerous world.

Summary: *This mystery puzzle is hereby given a possible solution. Ref. Neuroscience, Genetics, Cell biology*

How is our philosophical existence illusion of reality?

The philosophical existence illusion is also the new human's perceived technically altered true new reality.

The Observer's Reality - Miscellaneous notes

Notes: Page 82 – Figure 80 shows a 30-year-old hospital grade *Auto Blood Cell Analyzer* in which the book's author took part on the design of the electronic Red-White cell, Platelet processor, and numerous other PCB's to get it to the market during my working years in biotechnology cell analyzers R&D Elect. Eng. Dept.

Fig. 80a shows miscellaneous printed circuit boards with several PCB's of complex electronic designs for auto glucose portable meters done by the author ~10 years ago. Including smallest in the world at that time.

No. 80a –Modern Technology Glucose Meters

Note:
Human microbiome is composed of trillion cells. with a ~1:1.3 ratio vs. bacteria. For every human cell in our bodies there are ~1.3 bacterial organisms living in/out side our bodies in a symbiotic relationship specially in the gut, and they are required for our good health.

In reality, We are colonies of living walking dynamic ecosystems with some non-human cells. *Ref. Probiotics.*

Chapter X

Our temporary existence: The reality of life & death.

Human gut microbiome is composed of trillion of probiotic microorganisms.

Life as we know it contains specific combinations of the most common universal chemical elements which include: carbon, hydrogen, nitrogen, potassium, sodium, sulfur, phosphorus and oxygen. These elements combine to form proteins and nucleic acids which can replicate our DNA genetic code. Ref. pages 61-62- 63   **- No. 81 - Humans**

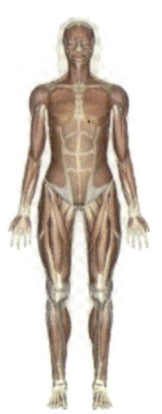

All basic atomic elements are formed in stars and distributed throughout space because of typical giant explosions called supernovas. Since these essential chemicals are quite common in other places in the biniverse, we can expect that the development of life somewhere else is also a possible natural evolutionary and very common chaotic universal evolution process.

Approx. 93% of humans' three basic elements are: carbon, oxygen, and hydrogen. Then approx. 6% are potassium, sodium, sulfur, phosphorus and nitrogen. Approximately 7% of the human genome is universal, and very similar to other mammals living in our planet.

Some genetic evolutionary interesting scientific facts are: Chimps' genetic code is approximately 99% identical to humans' genetic code. A banana's genetic code is approx. 65% identical to all human being's. Human's DNA may harbor ~145 bacteria, and viruses in the human genome that have become already part us.

No. 82 – DNA

No. 83 – Proteins    *All living organisms are strikingly similar at their molecular and cellular levels.* The basic physical unit of heredity is a linear sequence of nucleotides along a segment of DNA that provides the coded instructions for synthesis of RNA, which, when translated into proteins, leads to their genetic expression of hereditary characteristics that is controlled by these specialized unique cellular proteins.

Proteins give all living species the unique form of their physical appearance. Proteins are any of the numerous bio-organic 3D molecules constituting a large portion of the mass of every living form, composed of one or more long chains 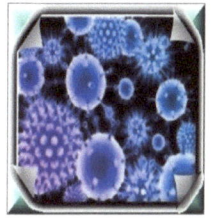 using the RNA messenger, and various enzymes by their chemical long 200 – 500 chain amino acid attachments.

No. 84 – Cells

Enzymes catalyze life chemical reactions RNA polymerase and synthesizes the formation of RNA from a DNA template during the genetic A<>T & C<>G molecular transcriptions of the digital respective life form of our biologically complex genetic code.

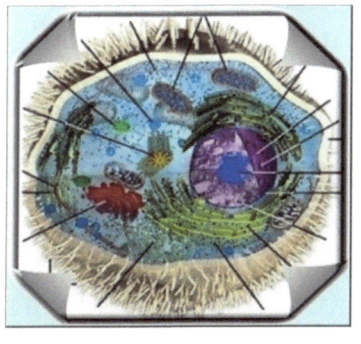

The basic elements of actual human cells are: ~65% Hydrogen, ~18% Carbon, ~3% Nitrogen, ~1% Phosphorus, and ~13% trace elements out of the well-known approx. 118 elements among which are: Iron, iodine, copper, zinc,

No. 85–Human-Cell -   fluoride, chromium, selenium, molybdenum, manganese, sulfur, calcium, potassium, and silicon among others. Etc. Ref. Elements page 48

The known universe is approximately 13.7 billion years as per the Big-Bang Theory. The planet Earth is approximately 4.5 billion years old. The first cells appeared on Earth about 3.5 billion years ago. So, you can basically see a natural evolution process taking place within a time window frame of about 9 billion years.

No. 86– Human Cells

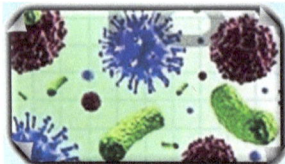

Living organisms require some energy sources to assimilate or put together the needed chemicals that form an individual. Energy is also required for the organism to grow, reproduce, and respond to their respective living environments.

Energy sources may include other organisms, light, or inorganic compounds. The most common source of energy on the planet Earth is sunlight. It is turned into usable energy through complex photosynthesis, which transforms sunlight into required food nutrients.

We can say that life is the natural emergence process of an ongoing electro-mechanical chemical biological evolutionary novel process using nanotechnology, and biogenetic auto-reproduction with self-repair genetic capability and almost perfect quality control of its cells.

The cell auto-epigenetic survival energetic process created across the entire planet can intelligently

No. 87–Gene's Info. Xfer.

replicate and evolve by natural chaotic revolutionary process of new adaptations to its constantly changing environment, and can pass survival genetic adaptive information to the future generations always trying to fulfill the mission to keep the evolutionary biological reproductive process going forward to improve it.

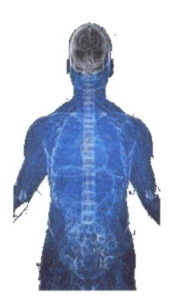
In other words, we humans seem to be programmable wet biological multicellular robotic organisms with approximately 250 different reproduced living human cells that are using a nanotechnological digital bio-genetic multi-codes of approximately 20,000 instructions within 46 biological DNA/RNA **No. 88- DNA** - chromosomes chains with biochemical memory storage capacity for static, and dynamic data microcontrollers using memory multiplexer system of x5 sensory parallel multi I/O input/output channelizer, bandwidth with multiple automatic systems, and auto-interconnected dual brain binary main bio-controllers.

Describing what I called the *Biniversal Law of Human's Life Existence: Life is the universal binary merging of a rare phenomenal sexually biogenetic transmitted syndrome onto two atypical living biological elemental basic cells, changing their natural genetic states into a new biological self-reproducing living organic cellular structure with a new encoded digital DNA molecularly inserted programmed genetic code.* RAZ Jr. - April 28, 2000 (Database). **No. 89- *DNA***

Once life's basic multi-elements are transformed into a biological living form, it becomes 100% terminal for the newly created organisms after running a normal DNA encoded digital multi-molecular programmed course of existence in the host species as a temporal emergence of life created into a biological multi-cellular new living organism capable of reproducing itself while trying to improve the best odds for the survival of the future generations to ensure the survival of their own species.

No. 90- *Universal Life* Transfer

The new created universal life syndrome is atypical on most extra special zones for habitable planetary environments and is created by the biniverse as one of a universal reality experience. Also, is used for the transfer of new genetic information, or as the means to improve chances of cell immortality. Specially for allowing the universe to experience its own multi-dimensional existence during the same temporal transitory evolutionary process of all living organisms that are as diverse, and numerous as the total of different celestial items found in the universe.

No. 91- DNA Genetic Transfer

The same above life's biniversal natural law of existence points to the fact that to be part of nature's chaotic universal creation once we do perform our function of passing our improved DNA-RNA genes transfer to the next new generation, we have by then already done or fulfilled our mission, and become expendable, since new improved life will become part of the updated, and enhanced new evolutionary future for better, and stronger generations.

The perception of a reality in which we will continue, an old-fashioned conservative way of seeing things must also become obsolete, since the old needs to be replaced by the new improved genetic versions, or by the new upgraded generations. Human cells are pre-programmed to die accordingly following this natural MTBF cells by the genetic telomere's controlled biogenetic process.

In a universe's life that is driven by an energy controlled efficient evolutionary system to select, and improve the survival of the fittest, and in **No. 92 Virus Life Forms -** which even stars eventually run out of fuel and die, it is only natural that most living organisms will eventually meet their (Minimum time before failure) death date. This MTBF at which time we all will reach the end of our journey in this universe and undergo a reverse transformation back into our basic elemental inert composition of natural elements, or recycled back into just the original energy as per M= E/C^2

From dust, you came, and to dust you shall return. - Genesis 3:19

We may not like this universal evolutionary process, but it is a fact. **No. 93 Death Tunnel** – Also there is nothing we can do about this process other than acceptance of our human true reality of our pre-programmed telomeres existence.

We can think about death as more real than life. It will help us if we look at it from a time-frame point of view. Non-existence was before life. Since death is non-existence, then we were dead since the known universe formed about 13.7 billion years ago. The Earth formed approx. ~4.5 billion years ago. The first cells appeared on Earth about 3.5 billion years ago. We were still dead. We're alive at present. But for a genetically pre-programmed very short time only. Enjoy it.

What is it like to be dead? Death is the termination of biological functions that sustain an organism's energy. Death cannot exist without life, and vice versa. It is a binary process. Life = 1 and Death = 0. This is the dual binary life reality of our existence in the universe as human beings. Ref. The X vs. Y Phase - Page 116 graph

While in the subject of our existence on Earth, and before we get on to the next chapter about the human brain, I want to challenge you to seek and embrace a new 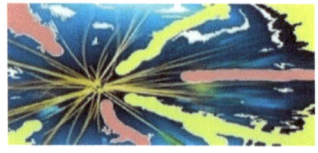 radical perception of true reality for our human brief existence versus an old limited view of the universe, or biniverse's Y phase **No. 94 Atomic Reality** – of the atomic energy reality.

Let us say that the binary 0 & 1 energy field was always there. Therefore, space had to always be there also for the energy field to exist in it. If we all agree that this is a viable possibility, then automatically the initial concept of time as in *always* is also created, as part of this equation in which they all merge to create existence. Energy, Space-Time: all 3 must exist at the same time. One cannot exist without the other two. But let us now...

Relate this concept to the mystery of the *Trinity* or the famous Einstein equation of: $E = MC^2$ and get your own conclusions to some different perceptions of true reality.

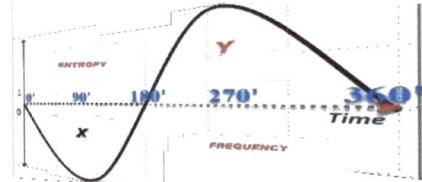 The way I see it is as follows: Energy always was in existence. But space-time emerged at **No. 95 Quantum Reality Energy** – the same time. So, there never was a beginning. We are in the Y wave cycle.

Now the real end for anything in existence will just be a quantum transition change of the physical properties in the above-mentioned dimensions of Energy, Space, and Time for the object in question. Until we can verify the existence of other dimensions as predicted by String Theory, and/or in quantum mechanics scientific fields, this is the reality we must live with, within the Y wave.

Furthermore, I also see the existence of planet Earth, which is the equivalent of a simple small grain of sand in the infinite vastness of the universe, as an existence that will come to an end. But will also be so insignificant to the universe's existence like us losing a grain of sand.

Granted is the fact that our *egos* may contradict these simple and factual points of view. In our ego's defense, I can also point to another scientific fact that there cannot exist two 100% identical objects in the universe, since this is an impossibility due to the chaotic entropy rules of the universe expansion, and the irreversible arrow of time controlling nature's entropy. *So, we all are unique...*

No. 96- half empty vs. half full glass

In other words, your perception of your universe, existence, and reality will never be 100% equal to the perception, existence, and reality of another human being's. We can have similar points of views, and/or just hope to be able to agree to disagree. Like the proverbial question: Is the glass half full or half empty?

The perception of reality is unique to every individual and is simply one's interpretation of our reality. Different perceptions can be correct at the same time just like particles can pop in - **No. 97–The cat** and out of existence, and/or two electrons exist at two different places at the same time, or to exist, and not to exist at some universal quantum frequency of existence is also another universal quantum reality of allowable probabilities in our "Q" binary existence.

In general physics, this is the principle that a wave-particle exists in the microphysics world of "Q" theory and both are complementary of each other creating reality only when measured, and/or when observed.

I love the game of chess. This is a game that I think everyone should learn to play during their lifetime.

Use it as a learning tool teacher to help you see problems, and all optional solutions from many different perspective options, alternatives, sacrifices, and/or the many possible game outcome options while following the complicated strict rules of the game.

The game is played on a square board of 8 x 8 squares with a total of 64 squares.

The legend about this game is that **No. 98–Chess -** King Shirham of India wanted to pay a request from the inventor of the game Vizier Sissa (a mathematician) requesting only that the king provided him with wheat grains equal to one grain in the 1st square, followed by two grains in the 2nd square, four grains in the third square, 8 grains in the fourth square, followed by 16, 32, 64, 128, 256, 512, 1,924 and so on in a geometrical progression until the 64 squares of board was accounted for as per his humble modest request....

To make a long story short, the king could not fulfill this promissory note, since to do so would have required 18,446,744,073,709,551,615 grains of wheat or a bag as large as the planet Earth. Rumor has it that Vizier Sissa's head was cut-off instead for his well calculated trickery.

As we can see the perception of reality is not obvious, and/or as simple as we may think at first sight, before we look, see, observe, and analyze the situation from all possible different angles and diverse points of view.

<u>**Summary:**</u> *This mystery puzzle is hereby given a possible solution. Ref. Neuroscience, Genetics, Biology.*

How is our reality of temporary life & death existence?

Life & death realities of our temporary existence inside the human's life forms are mostly gigantic virtual egos.

The Observer's Reality - Miscellaneous notes

No. 98a – Chess game board set-up

No. 98b – Chess clock

There are computers that can easy outperform any human playing a chess game using AI – Artificial Intelligence.

Deep Blue is one. But down at component level computers are binary electronic devices switching 0's and 1's with Boolean transistor gates at high speed, using software languages that eventually are compiled back to the machine binary language, and math of simple binary numbers of only 0's & 1's. This is what is going on in the computerized world even for artificial intelligence.

The algorithms, and designs used by nature, or the so called *intelligent designs* points to the facts that any technological human's breakthrough inventions are just poor imitations of an already existing, and much better design found in nature and done by *"evolution"* alone.

We need to accept the fact that all awesome heavenly things we see in nature are God's energy creations, done by *evolution* using all energies to create the *intelligent designs* that we admire and find terrific mind-blowing. But let us not forget that chaos is also part of this creation in the biniverse, and just like good things get created, so are bad ones that we fear, try to avoid and keep away to avoid harm. But we cannot do it forever…

Chapter XI

The Brain: The receptor & decoder of our own sensory-perceived physical, and virtual 4-D realities.

The human brain is probably the most mysterious, interesting, and complex object within our universe to use and take full advantage of during our short lives.

No. 99 – "Q" Brain   Some interesting brain facts are:

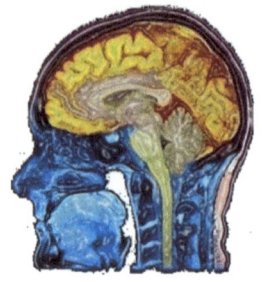

Our brain is the human organ that interprets the reality of our existence, the real perception of our awareness of being here and present. It does this interfacing directly with our sensory and nervous systems, decoding and interpreting all external, and internal electro-chemical physical stimuli received in the form of changing electrical voltages, currents, temperature, air, light, physical pressure, and changes in frequencies.

It interprets reality using neurotransmitter molecular detection cells, to recall short and long-term memories of previous knowledge and all of our life's experiences.

No. 100 – Brain Neurons

There are some very strange and beautiful comparisons between the human brain and the universe. I am hereby one of many people proposing a connection between the structure of the universe and the structure of the human" Q" brain.

As we have previously seen, the brain's neuron formations, and the structure of the known universe's cluster of all galaxies distributions are comparable visually. The fact is that the universe and the brain, by strange coincidence, look very much like each other.

The visible known universe is ~95% hydrogen. The human body is ~65% hydrogen, ~18% carbon, ~3% nitrogen, ~1% phosphorus, and another ~13% trace elements like: iron, iodine, fluoride, copper, zinc, sulfur, chromium, molybdenum, selenium, manganese, calcium, potassium, silicon. Etc. All atomic elements are created by and are part of the same universe or biniverse equivalents.

No.101–Universe-Biniverse

This makes one wonder since we are created by it, if every human brain is just a small microscopic imitation of the structure of the dynamic universe.

Or if it just created a finger print image of it on each of us. We are all created to the image, and similarity of our creator, and you just cannot deny this fact. We seem to be a fractal like expansion of the changing biniverse.

The universe seems to keep a wireless and indirect communication interface with us using all forces of nature, different energies, and sometimes I wonder if the quantum entanglement phenomenon also applies to this "*mysterious quantum linkage*" across distant space-time.

But when we look at the fractal phenomenon, or the living cells, seeds, the photon in a hologram; they all contain the requirements to recreate the whole from a single unity or a singularity point. They all have this very strange, but beautiful similarity. If we observe other phenomena like a black hole, or quantum extra dimensions to add more food or additional ingredients to the primordial soup of the creation, or just food for thought. Then we can look, see, and observe for the digital fingerprints left behind by the creator for us to analyze, study, and try to understand the unknown incredibly amazing world that is presented before our Q sensory 4-D detection systems.

The theories that everything was created from a single energy point, that everything is interconnected and that all comes from the same root in the universal natural world seems to be proven by our observations.

No. 102 – A virtual view of the known universe

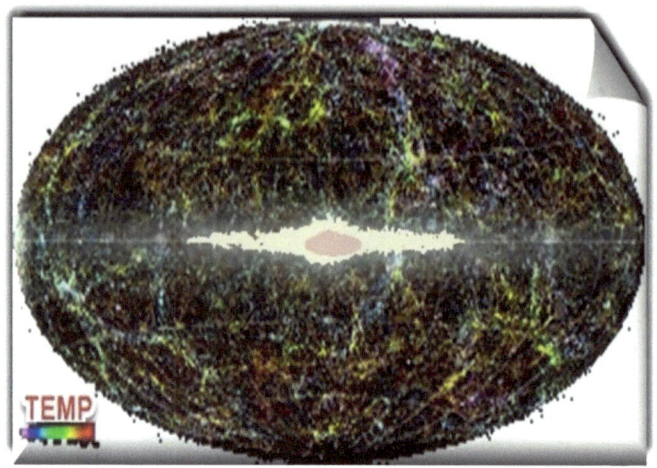

Note: Additional facts about the "Q" similarities between the universe and the human brain:

The typical brain has approximately 100 billion brain cells that equals approx. 100 trillion brain connections synapses which also are the same approx. number of stars in the known universe. Also, we have approx. 100 trillion cells in the human body which are also the approx. number of stars in the known atomic Q universe.

Add to it the fact that we are also made of the same components found in the universe, since the basic elements humans are made of are: hydrogen, carbon, oxygen, sulfur, and phosphorus. Then you can draw your own conclusions about these elemental fraternities.

The above facts sure do make us wonder about coincidences that seem to point to an original single root of our evolutionary universal Q creation as a fractal fact.

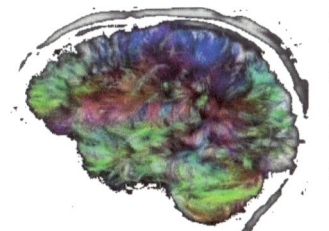

No. 103 - Brain connectivity and neuron's mapping
Brain cellular neurological structure information

It is well known that biological living cells first appeared on Earth about 3.5 billion years ago. Presently there are approx. 350 different human cells that are controlled by a double-helix molecular interlaced chain linked with approx. 100 to 500 different 23 amino acids protein molecules named: A/T & C/G for A = Adenine, C = Cytosine, G = Guanine, and T = Thymine molecule. Ref. DNA molecular attraction.

This molecular biological cell structure of our own complex genetic DNA / RNA chromosomes uses Nano-technology, and high-speed meiosis duplication process to reproduce the genetic information in the production of new fast regenerative cell production during regular maintenance process of all living biologic organisms.

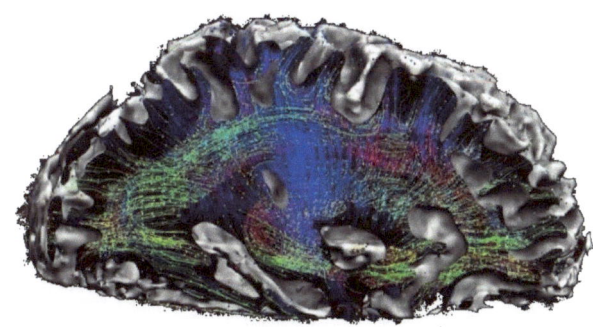

No. 104 Brain Internal View

Summary: This mystery puzzle is hereby given a possible solution. Ref. Neuroscience, Genetics, Biology.

How is our Brain the receptor & decoder of our own sensory - perceived physical, and virtual 4-D realities?

The reality of our life existence and perception is created by our own brains using electro-chemical stimuli on our ~100 billion neurons and nervous system cells.

The Observer's Reality - Miscellaneous notes

Notes: Before going into the last chapter I would like to help clarify how complicated things including the whole biniverse, can still be done with simple 0's &1's or - / + binary systems. Ref. Author's Binary "Q" Graph.

If you are awed by computers, then you can see the power of the binary system math done with 0's and 1's.

Every multi-complex electronic function at their component level are performed at high speed controlled by a master crystal clock. All highly integrated solid state devices on the different electronic modules only see those 2 binary states of a 1 or 0 - On or off – Energized, or non-energized. The system of Boolean algebra using transistorized highly integrated solid state logic gates.

Now visualize a 3D binary printer using above technology to print-out living organs as it can be done today to help you see the power of binary systems.

Ref. to page 68, 128. We need to understand that the universe using all types of different energies like kinetic, potential, thermal, light, chemical, electrical, sound, mechanical, electrochemical, electromagnetic, nuclear, and dark energy among others with unlimited time, and using evolution fractals, natural algorithms, random chaos, with entropy, can eventually create what some people call *intelligent designs*, and others call a normal evolutionary processes taking place controlled by fractals and mother nature laws using algorithms driven by energy efficiency binary processes.

Also, if we *"observe"* carefully, all the different variables are factors of the same equations of creation.

They are not different, and can co-exist with each other. *No Issues.* It is just a *perception* thing…vs. *egos.*

Chapter XII

Summary *and conclusions to the mysteries of our existence, and philosophical possible probabilities for solutions to the unknown mysterious puzzles of life.*

The following are additional informative and technical notes to help illustrate the ideas presented in the field of astrophysics, chemistry, physics, math, quantum physics biology, neuroscience, metaphysics, spiritual human philosophy, atomic sub-particles, time, space, energy forces, gravity, bio-genetics and neurotheology among others which are required to be able to see *true* reality.

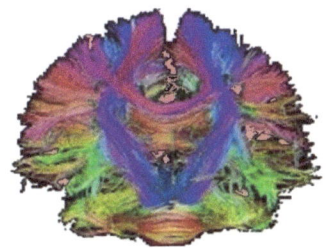

Once you clearly understand the material covered in these topics, you will either enjoy this book, or disagree with my radical points of view. Also, it will help if you are extra curious to the book's provided information links.

No. 105 – Brain Neuron's View - "Internet hyperlinks".

The main purpose of this book is to try to explain the myths, legends, puzzles, mysteries and phenomena providing possible solutions, or probabilities to the interested layperson. Ref. Author's Binary Biniverse Graph.

Since most of the topics covered by this book are controversial and radical, many readers will disagree with the ideas presented. They will classify them as pseudo-science, and/or science-fiction without any supporting scientific evidence in addition to: $E = M*C^2$.

I am okay with that. I know I am thinking outside the box and hope there is some truth to these radical and controversial theories described in this book in a very simplistic law of "Q" probabilities compact manner.

Keeping in mind that the topics addressed by this book are complex, and scientific in nature, and in most cases depending in the reader's knowledge of the subject matter - may be easy or difficult to understand. *Resource hyperlinks* to related material is provided for the benefit, and convenience of the reader who wants to dig deeper into the ideas covered by this interesting informative metaphysics book. Google it is an option. Ref. page 121.

No. 106 –Earth's Internet Connectivity View
Internet of Things - Social media - Online reality

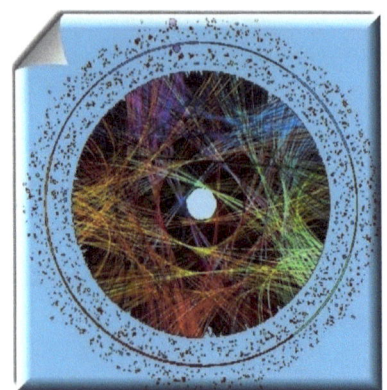

Wi-Fi ® - Bluetooth® - ISP e-mail - Google® - Twitter® Cable TV - Facebook® - YouTube® - Smart Phones – Apps - iPad® - Computers - IBM ® - Netflix® - Spam - PC Hacking - Browsers – Cookies - Instagram® - ID's Anti-virus – Virtual Reality.

Technical notes: Additional research to get more familiar with some of the above terms, and or ideas tackled in this book can be made in the *internet of things*.

Terms like Singularity, Binary systems, Fractals, Virtual reality, NASA-Hubble, Hologram, and Quantum physical entanglement should trigger your curiosity into the field of astrophysics, quantum physics, general physics, biology, the quantum binary systems, and metaphysics to name a few. The most interesting subject covered in this book however is our human "Q" brain.

There is a proverb that goes: *"Ignorance is very daring."* With my limited life's knowledge, and experience I dared to write a book explaining some important mysteries of life, and our human *true* reality.

But we know that at present time the popular "Think Tanks" in their brainstorming of intellectual analytical group techniques take advantage of the so called "wisdom of the crowds". In these think tanks, laypersons take part in a specialized group of experts from a field to try to find and solve a complex problems, enigmas, phenomena or mysteries needing difficult solutions.

The outsider is not biased by the technical field knowledge, and can see the problem, and possible solutions from a completely different point of view that the experts will continually miss due to their brain programming that keeps them locked "inside the box" of knowledge of their respective fields, with restricting tunnel vision vs. the typical layperson's open mind.

No. 107 – Brain Activity View

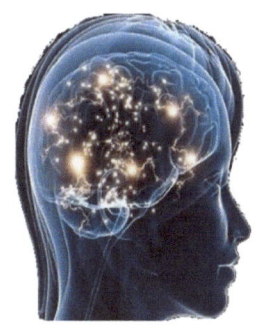

Another good simple way of finding some solutions to complex problems is to give your problem to your brain to solve it. The brain loves to find the correct answers, and solve complex problems. But most importantly, it is a tool that has being improving to do this task for billions of years. And it is at your disposal. Use it or lose it. Force it to make new neural pathway connections using *neuroplasticity* with epic-genetics to reprogram it, improve it, and keep it sharp. Provide it with plenty of water, physical/mental exercises to take good care of it.

Please refer to Chapter VIII – Page 76 to find solutions to mysteries within the brain, since it is directly connected via wireless interfaces to the universe by the mysterious phenomena of quantum entanglement across space-time multidimensional biniverse distances.

Listen to your body is good advice. But asking the brain to think, analyze, and solve your problems is a more logical and better strategic piece of advice. It has been doing that to keep us alive for billions of years. Yes, that is how old this wonderful tool at your disposal is.

It is the most dynamic organ in your body, it changes every day. Use your intelligence, creativity, and your brain for good! It can also be a very dangerous tool when used against its natural positive bias of cosmic harmony.

Who are we? The basic elements of human's cells are approx. 65% Hydrogen, 18% Carbon, 3% Nitrogen, 1% Phosphorus, 13% trace elements among which are: iron, iodine, copper, zinc, fluoride, sulfur, chromium, silicon. manganese, molybdenum, calcium, and potassium, etc.

The three basic requirements for living cells on Earth to exist, and be able to thrive are:

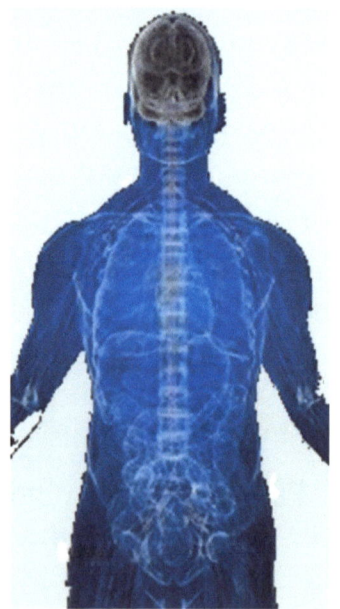

1. Liquid Water: H_2O Composed of 2 hydrogens and 1 oxygen atom.

2. Essential Chemicals: Described above. (Who are we)?

3. Energy Sources: Our sun, gravity, atomic nuclear radiation, and other electromagnetic and biochemical energies.

No. 108 – Brain connectivity view

For life cells to exist and thrive they must also be able to perform the following:

A. Use energy sources for their metabolism, organic matter, and chemicals. (Survival).

B. Can grow, reproduce, and transfer their cell genetic organization information. (Reproduction).

C. Survive through proper response to environmental stimuli by efficient adaptation to daily chaotic encounters, and evolve with new survival adaptations by beneficial genetic mutations. (Adaptability).

No. 109 – Cell Communications - Ref. pages 18 & 19

The mitochondrion is an example of the genetic cell energy efficiency adaptation.

This is a spherical or elongated organelle in the cell cytoplasm of nearly all eukaryotic cells, containing genetic material and many enzymes important for cell metabolism, including those responsible for the conversion of food and provide usable organism's high energy supplies.

It is also called chondriosome. It was incorporated into our human cells billions of years ago for energy efficiency, and survival of the fittest advantage.

Chondriosome DNA is different than humans' DNA.

If we were created by the universe, and we are part of universe being aware of its own existence by using our sensory organic perceptions, the universe can become the observer creating our virtual reality of our existence.

In a fractal way, it is the universe's own existence using different multiple types of life forms to be the observer. Ref. http://www.nbcnews.com/science/8-8-billion-habitable-earth-size-planets-exist-milky-way

Without these different types of external observers to detect biniversal cause and effect, the universe will be unable to experience its own existence and just be an energy singularity with no time, space, or life in it.

Therefore, energy must create matter, and this matter must expand, and become bio-organic living material as the universal law of existence states. Universal life is a natural requirement for the universe to be aware of its existence following the famous equation of Einstein's Theory of Relativity ($E = MC^2$) and *The Biniversal Law of human life existence.* RAZ Jr. - Reference Page 87.

Back in the first chapter we said that the key question was not *who?* but <u>*how?*</u> *How* will give us the answer. If after reading this book and learning about <u>*how*</u> everything took place, you still need to search for *who*, then please do so. But *how* will yield an ampler search.

No. 110 – Brain Mind Awareness Activity

If we think or feel that the mystery of existence needs to start only from a *mystical* beginning, that we also need a starting point (in which initially there was *nothing* - no time, no space, no energy). All this before there was any existence. If we can only see it as a spiritual holy entity, or a divine presence that created everything in complete control of existence of the uncreated, or of a non-existing biniverse energy. We must respect the "blind faith" point of views.

The alternative <u>chaos</u> described by the contents of this metaphysics book will help to see it otherwise different as per the author's Biniverse Graph showing and initial binary energy radiation field with a quantum emergence.

If you use faith, please stay with it. There is nothing wrong with different points of view. As the observer of my own reality, I see the biniverse as our creator. But you are also an observer. You can also see a different reality, and/or have a human right to live by "blind faith".

No. 111 – Brain Mind Awareness

What do you think you are seeing? Always look, see, observe, analyze, and understand to be able to try to comprehend. *Plato* said we cannot see reality. But *Aristotle* said we can. Both were right, and both were wrong. They were best friends, and just respectfully agreed to disagree on their different points of view.

They did not allow their differences to separate them. But instead used their differences to enjoy each other's company. Their different points of views allowed the diversity of thoughts to enrich their lives and even our lives. The different ideas bringing them closer as friends.

Enlightenment means to embrace non-attachment, and non-judgement of our egos with acceptance for the impermanent chaotic nature and non-existence of the physical past or uncontrollable uncertain future reality, since this will allow us to live only in the present moment in space-time, while we breath out all our human suffering and negative energy, and breath in positive joy, and happiness to share it with the people forming our large entire humanity's circle of empathic love.

No. 112 – The "Q" Brain-Mind Observer

We can sense only what our brains tell us we see, hear, smell, touch, or taste, and this is not always true...

Live your life, and enjoy your loves. Keep life simple, and always be willing to compromise to get a win-win agreement. Keep in mind that real happiness must emerge from within us. Enjoy it to add to it. But share it to multiply it. RAZ Jr.

No. 113 – The Beauty of Nature

Remember...there are no simple things in life, only limited points of view. People will interpret simple things in numerous different ways. If I say to you: Nothing is simple, then I'll be contradicting myself. See why?

So, trying to solve the "puzzles" was by no means easy. But it sure was a lot of fun! I hope you enjoyed this radical, controversial, new book about metaphysics as I did looking for the answers to solve some of the puzzles, mysteries, and/or phenomena that describes true reality.

<u>Summary</u>: This mystery puzzle is hereby given a possible solution. Ref. Philosophy, Neuroscience, Genetics.

How is our universe and human existence explained?

The Biniverse created our existence by a binary chaotic quantum emergence. Then evolution made us The Observers of Reality. The End & The Beginning.

Or maybe it is only just another probability....

Epilogue

During the process of writing this informative metaphysics book, I read many technical materials, watched videos and TV programs, and researched lots of related material to compile and reach conclusions for this informative and educational book. I provided the readers a small condensed book of all my findings on true reality.

I also conducted research online to provide readers with the most up-to-date information on all material. I consider a good informative learning book one that can be a life changing upon reading it. This is my goal, and I hope "The Observer's Reality" is one that will teach you to see reality in a different, radical, and bold new ways.

DB No. 114 – Database's complex structure

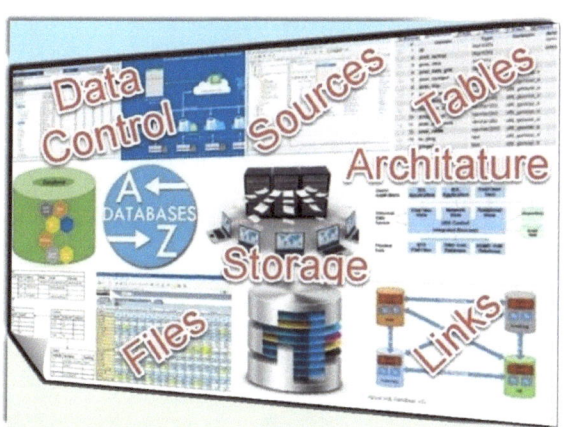

The related information for writing this book was also collected during many, many years....

I entered all data in a large P&V Database while searching all the answers to this book's well described mysteries or puzzles of natural phenomena.

It is with great pleasure that I am finally willing to put it all together, and share this information with my family, friends, and other curious readers. I am hereby writing a memoir of my life time learnings in this compact format. The Observer's Reality became a project during my well-deserved transition of working life into retirement.

Afterword

One of the challenges of this book was to keep the complexity of the material as clear, but also compact as possible, showing all the possible sides of a "Q" binary system. Things can be as simple as nothing = 0, and or as complex as everything = 1 departing from a middle reference line. - *No. 115 – Atomic Particles*

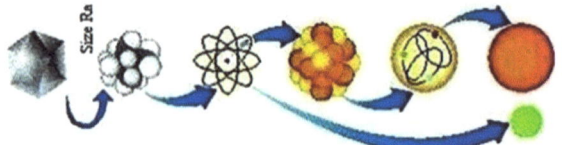

Acquiring scientific knowledge, and philosophical wisdom, and or enlightenment depends on how much you are motivated, and how willing you are to dig deep into the rabbit's hole, *into the unknown,* always keeping in mind that impossible may be a limiting factor and or maybe just in this presently known biniverse/universe.

But if you have more time, well then the multiverses probability (with new more exotic dimensions) are waiting for your string theory curiosity. Be my guest, and go for it. It will be fun, and read lots of interesting books!

No. 116 – String Theory Math

2.2.3 Varying $\tilde{S}_0$ in an Arbitrary Background (Geodesic Equation)

If we choose the parameter τ in such a way that the auxiliary field $e(\tau)$ takes the value $e(\tau) = 1$, then the action $\tilde{S}_0$ becomes

$$\tilde{S}_0 = \frac{1}{2}\int d\tau \left(g_{\mu\nu}(X)\dot{X}^\mu \dot{X}^\nu - m^2\right). \quad (2.20)$$

Now, if we assume that the metric is not flat, and thus depends on its spacetime position, then varying $\tilde{S}_0$ with respect to $X^\mu(\tau)$ results in

$$\delta \tilde{S}_0 = \frac{1}{2}\int d\tau \left(2g_{\mu\nu}(X)\delta\dot{X}^\mu \dot{X}^\nu + \partial_k g_{\mu\nu}(X)\dot{X}^\mu \dot{X}^\nu \delta X^k\right)$$

$$= \frac{1}{2}\int d\tau \left(-2\dot{X}^k \partial_k g_{\mu\nu}(X)\delta X^\mu \dot{X}^\nu - 2g_{\mu\nu}(X)\delta X^\mu \ddot{X}^\nu + \delta X^k \partial_k g_{\mu\nu}(X)\dot{X}^\mu \dot{X}^\nu\right)$$

$$= \frac{1}{2}\int d\tau \left(-2\ddot{X}^\nu g_{\mu\nu}(X) - 2\partial_k g_{\mu\nu}(X)\dot{X}^k \dot{X}^\nu + \partial_\mu g_{k\nu}(X)\dot{X}^k \dot{X}^\nu\right)\delta X^\mu.$$

Setting this variation equal to zero gives us the field equations for $X^\mu(\tau)$ in an arbitrary background, namely

$$-2\ddot{X}^\nu g_{\mu\nu}(X) - 2\partial_k g_{\mu\nu}(X)\dot{X}^k \dot{X}^\nu + \partial_\mu g_{k\nu}(X)\dot{X}^k \dot{X}^\nu = 0, \quad (2.21)$$

which can be rewritten as

$$\ddot{X}^\mu + \Gamma^\mu_{kl}\dot{X}^k \dot{X}^l = 0, \quad (2.22)$$

https://math.berkeley.edu/~kwray/papers/string_theory.pdf

Conclusion

This informative metaphysics book is dense with syntheses of radical, and controversial new ideas. It liberates itself from the standard layout template of seeing most of our own perception of everything in a different unconventional way, with a new challenging breakthrough paradigm for human knowledge on our reality, or in other words let us get real if it is possible.

Written with remarkable insight that sometimes provides breathtaking arguments for anyone seeking answers to the most profound life mysteries that challenge our capacity to understand the hypothesis of everything seeing from other conceivable view angles.

No. 117 – Optional possibilities

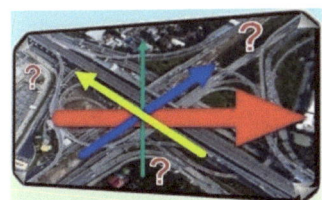

I welcome readers' critiques of my arguments. These pages contain radical unconventional new possible solutions, and ideas to the deciphering of phenomena.

It offers new possible objective answers to many mysteries in astrophysics, astronomy, biology, life, evolution, the uni/biniverse, quantum physics, atoms, particles, sub-atomic particles and the more interesting mysteries of our true reality of biological existence of our life, and the guaranteed eventual MTBF deaths.

In the field of neuroethology, we find some of the questions to which I will like to find clearer and better explanations using both science and philosophy.

These were the virtual illusions and mysteries of the beginning of time, space limits, eternity, infinity, realities of death, chaos, entropy, energy, matter, life, biological cancer cells, brain vs. mind virtual creations. and expected big crunch End at the Y phase bottom...

Reviewing 3 requirements for life to exist:

1. Liquid Water Molecules: Two hydrogen atoms + 1 oxygen atom. Liquid water H_2O is essential because biochemical reactions take place in water.

2. Essential Chemicals: Carbon, hydrogen, nitrogen, oxygen, and phosphorous. Life as we know it typically contains specific combinations of elements including carbon, hydrogen, nitrogen, and oxygen that combine to form proteins and nucleic acids which can replicate DNA-RNA biological genetic code for cell reproduction.

3. Energy Source: Organisms require energy to assimilate or put together the chemicals that form an individual. Energy is also needed for the organism to grow, reproduce, and respond to the environment.

No. 118 – Energy – Matter – Time & Space

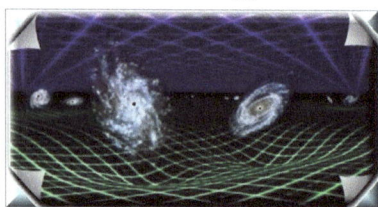

Metaphysics the branch of philosophy, and scientific human knowledge of our intellect, that examines the nature of reality, including the relationship between mind and matter, substance and attribute, fact and value as a probability of our unique binary universal existence inside the existing energy – matter – space -time - biniverse sinewave graph cycle.

No. 119 – The known biniverse distribution

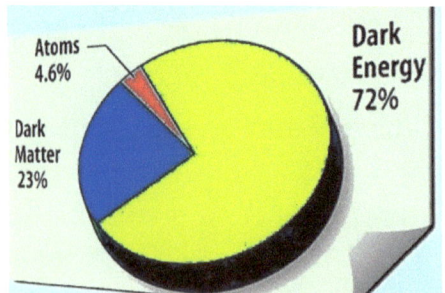

Approximately only 5% is the "observable" atomic matter universe. Per $M = E / C^2$ formula.

The other 95% of it is presently unknown as shown per graph.

Postscript

Additional information appended to the book as final notes providing related knowledge as part of the story, and or main point of this informative book.

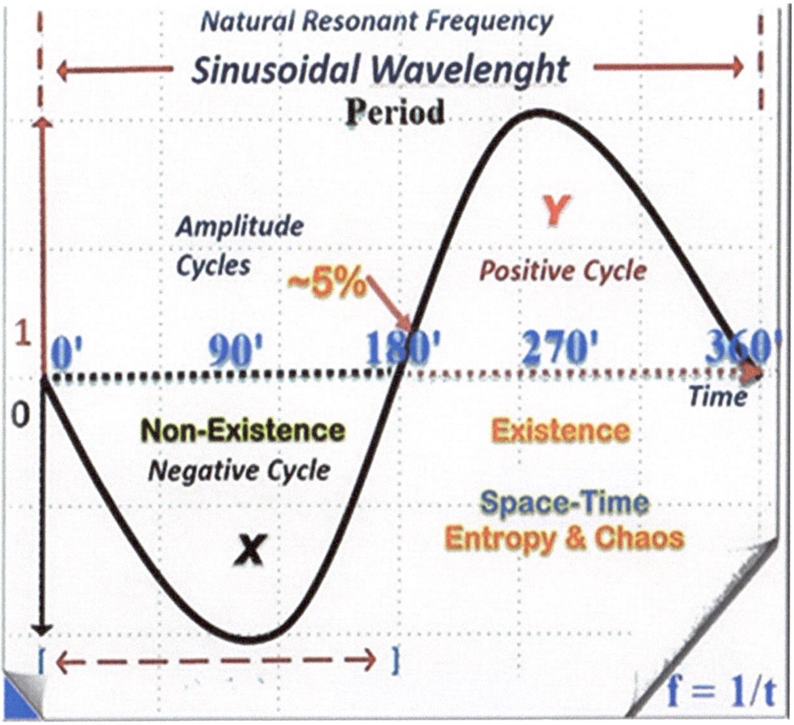

No. 2b Biniverse Graph - Energy – Space – Time

Sinewave formulas: A sinB ((0 -C) +D   Y= Sin X

A sinewave or sinusoid is a mathematical curve that describes a smooth repetitive oscillation. It is named after the function sine.

In a right triangle, the sine of an angle is the length of the opposite side divided by the length of the hypotenuse. Ref. pages: 3, 113, 119, 122, 126.

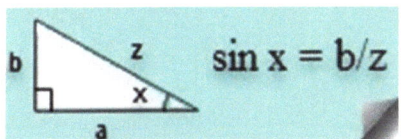 *No. 2c - Biniverse Graph*

Glossary

Binary System: Mathematical Numeric System with Base 2 (0 & 1). In a binary quantum system, natural entanglements of duality interconnecting communication interfaces the state of 1 factor will automatically determine the other Binary 0 or 1.

Basic Requirements for Life: The first cells appeared on Earth about 3.5 billion years ago. The three basic requirements for life on Earth: 1. Liquid Water 2. Essential Chemicals 3. Energy Source

Energy: 4 major known sources of universal forces: Gravity, Electro-Magnetic, Nuclear, & Weak (Radiation) Energy.

Galaxies: A system of stars independent from all other systems. The Milky Way galaxy is where our Solar system, sun, & 12 planets (8 planets and 4 dwarf planets) exist. The distance across our galaxy is 100,000 light years.

Hydrogen: The gaseous mass that surrounds any planet, including Earth. A hydrogen atom a big piece of positive energy (proton) connected to a small piece of negative energy (electron). In this binary universe ~ 95% are hydrogen atom and only ~ 5% is visible matter at present time. Energy generators for life supporting of planets.

Kinetic Energy: Potential energy, Thermal, or Heat Energy - Chemical - Electrical - Electrochemical - Electromagnetic Energy light - Photons. Sound, Chemical, Radiant, Electric, Atomic and Mechanical - Nuclear - Dark - Weak.

Life: Digital life is a biological phenomenon, and a mystery. The first cells appeared on Earth about 3.5 billion years ago. Presently there are 350 different human cells. Cells are humans' basic elements. They are made of ~18% Carbon, ~65% Hydrogen, ~ 3% Nitrogen, ~1% Phosphorus, ~13% trace elements, Sulfur, Iron, etc.

Nothing: Is an impossibility. In a "Q" binary system 0 & 1 are only temporary-state transitions of energy values at the frequency of reality in our perceived biniverse existence as per author's sinewave biniverse theory cycle shown graphically. References Page 122.

Glossary

Planets: A large, nonluminous mass, usually with its own moons, which revolve around a star. Planets are found everywhere in the galaxy. Planets must have enough gravity mass so that its own gravity force shapes it into a spherical body. Planets have two requirements:
a) It must have enough mass for self-gravity to overcome normal rigid-body forces to assume hydrostatic equilibrium. In other words, they must be nearly round by gravity force. Ref. *Higgs Boson*
b) Orbits around a star, and is not a satellite of another planet.

Our Solar System: The Sun; Inner Planets: **1.** Mercury- both hottest and coldest, no rotation 2. Venus- gaseous, diameter of 12,100 kilometers **3.** Earth- water and solid **4.** Mars- solid, some ice (perhaps water) planets: **5.** Jupiter- ongoing storm/red spot **6.** Saturn- ring **7.** Uranus- vertical stand / Ref. other planets - **8.** Neptune-gaseous planet **9.** Pluto - a demoted planet. Pluto's moon Charon.

Albert Einstein Theory of Relativity which states that energy equals matter times speed of light squared.
$$E=MC^2 \text{ or } M = E / C^2 \text{ and } C = \sqrt{E/M}$$

Quantum Tunneling Effect of Emergence: The Quantum Tunneling Effect of Emergence of sub-atomic particles created the effect of the big bang of the universe, and stars use the same quantum tunneling effect to create atoms, matter, and energy.

Stars: Are hydrogen to helium atomic fusion energy generators. There are approximately 200 to 400 billion stars in the Milky Way galaxy, and about 10 billion trillion stars in the universe. Stars serve as the natural life supporting energy source of any planet.

Universe/Biniverse: The **binary universe** ~95% of atoms are hydrogen atoms, and ~5% visible matter. There are ~10 billion trillion stars in the universe and ~200 to 400 billion stars in the Milky Way.

Reality: What we perceive as particles atoms or matter are only vibrations or strings of energy. Fields that pervade all of space at a time or oscillating resonant "Q" frequency to create our perceived existence. Ref. Sinewave curve cycle shown - **References Pages 111 & 116.**

Glossary
No. 120 - Life Timeline

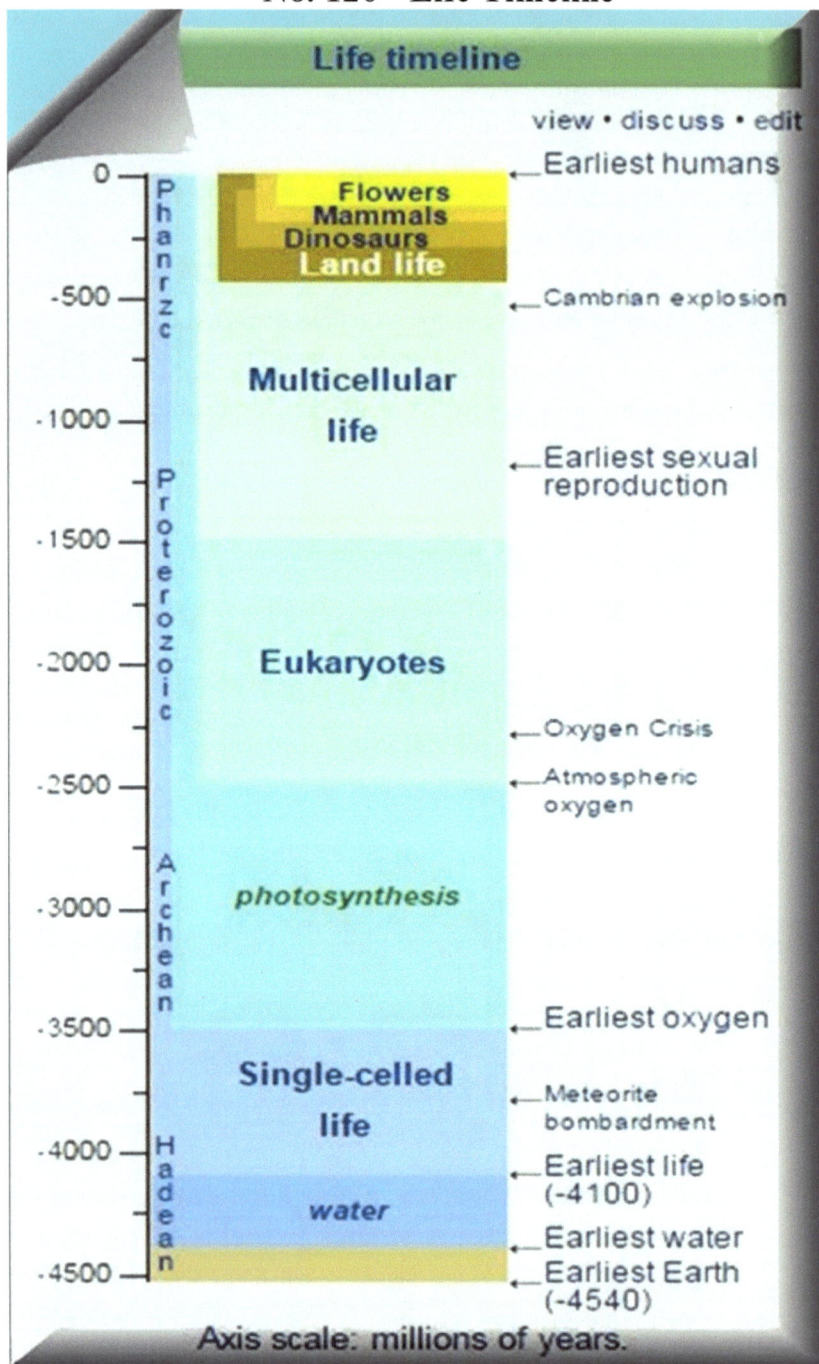

Glossary

List of Earth minerals: Aluminum, Antimony, Carbon, Chromium, Cobalt, Copper, Gold, Iron Hafnium, Lead, Magnesium, Golden White Manganese, Molybdenum, Nickel, Niobium Palladium, Platinum, Rhenium, Selenium, Silver, Tantalum, Tellurium, Tin, Titanium, Tungsten, Vanadium, Zinc, and Zirconium.

List of Alloys used for coins and medals: Acmonital, Aluminum, Bronze, Argentan, Barton's Metal, Bath Metal, Bell Metal, Billon, Brass, Bronze = Copper + Tin, Crown Gold, Cupro-Nickel, Dowmetal Electrum, Franklinium, German Silver, Gun Metal, Manganese Bronze, Nickel Brass, Nickel Silver, Nordic Gold, Orichalchum, Pewter, Pinchbeck, Potin, Silver Alloys, Speculum, Stainless Steel. Steel = Iron - Without (Carbon), Tombac, Virenium, White Metal. Etc.

Non-Metals used for currency: Carbon, Clay, Fiber, Glass, Leather, Paper, Plastic, Porcelain, Selenium, Silicon, and Stone.

Crystals: A crystal is a material whose constituents, such as atoms, molecules or ions, are arranged in a highly ordered microscopic structure like the fractals symmetrical distributions. Many living biological organisms can produce organ-genic crystals.

Crystallization: Is the process of forming a crystalline structure from a fluid or from materials dissolved in a fluid. There are four types of crystals: covalent, metallic, molecular and ionic.

Glossary

Albert Einstein 1879-1955 Theory of relativity $E=MC^2$
Biniverse *Graph - Energy – Space – Time*

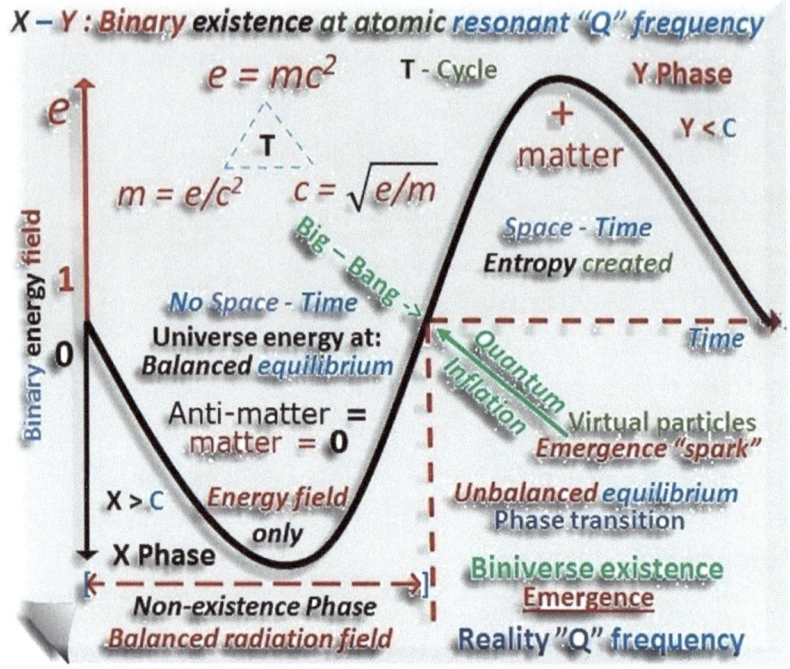

No. 121 - Biniverse Theory by: RAZ Jr.
Ref.   Pages: 113, 119, 122, 126.

August 17, 2008

Sinewave formulas: A sinB ((0 -C) +D   Y= Sin X

A sinewave or sinusoid is a mathematical curve that describes a smooth repetitive oscillation. It is named after the function sine. **Ref.   Pages: 122, 126.**

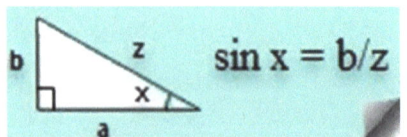

No. 2c - Biniverse Graph

Glossary

No. 122- Biniverse Expansion

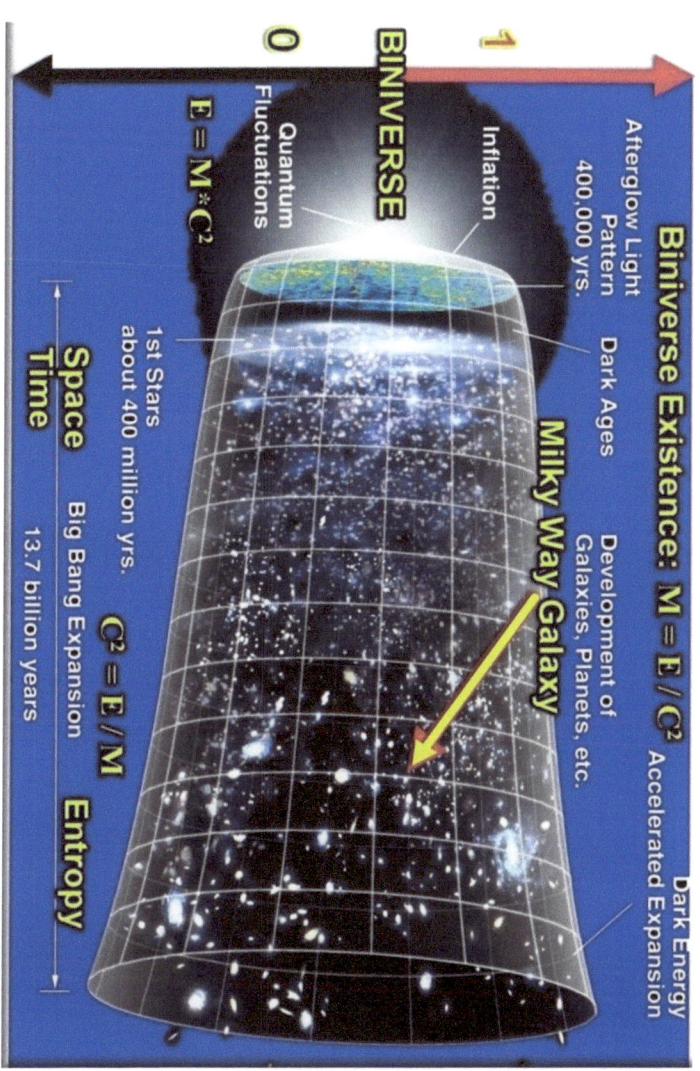

The Big Bang theory vs. a possible quantum binary phase transition emergence implosion from 0 to 1 creating space & time during the transition in very similar way that sub-atomic particles pop in, and out of existence creating an *unbalanced expanding "Biniverse."*

Glossary

No. 123- Life Evolution

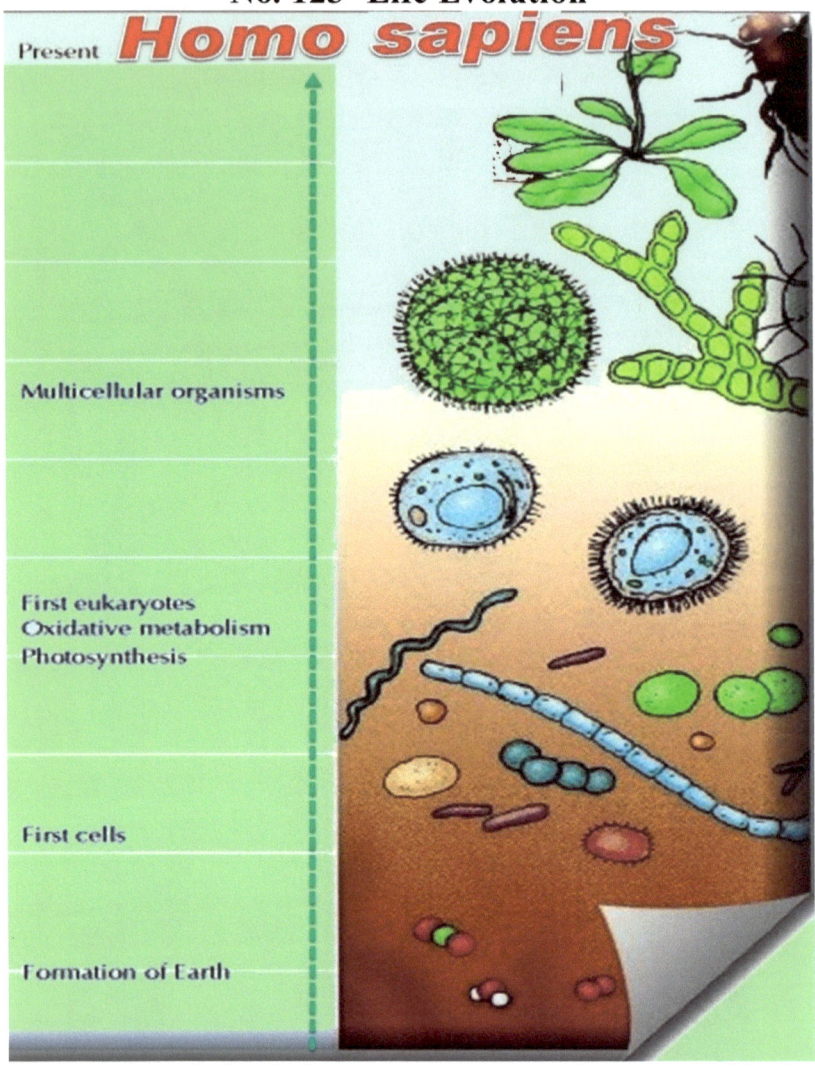

Note: Research on appendixes A - B - C, and reference topics will help the layperson reader to better understand the ideas, and topics presented in this book. Additionally, please feel free to conduct your own online research to aid you in your understanding of the material using *http://www.google.com* with page 130 keywords.

The Observer's Reality - Miscellaneous notes

Notes:

Q. How does the author prove his theory of an ongoing constant sinewave binary changing biniverse cycle (As per his Binary Theory Graph)? Ref. Page 116 - Fig. 121.

A. The influence of this constant sinewave cycle at the frequency of entropy will prevent the 100% perfect duplication of any object created in the universe at atomic level. Objects can look, and be functional equivalents. But reproduction, and or duplication can never be anatomically identical due to this described entropy effect. This may provide the evidence for the argument's assertion as a true probability. RAZ Jr.

Everything in the universe is unique. Similar but never identical due to *entropy*. Ref. LUCA at page 57.

So, when we finally implement the, "beam me up Scotty" teleportation idea, keep in mind that there will be some atomic degradation in your body after each use.

And now you also know of another contributing factor of why we age daily, when our dying cells get replaced.

Additional related *important* final information follows in the next pages, please continue until the end at page 137.....Yes, our *"suffering"* is almost over.... ☺

Bibliography

Bibliography and reference sections listed below show the reference sources used during the writing of this book arranged in order of reference priority and/or alphabetical order.

All topics, and subjects covered by this informative metaphysics book, "The Observer's Reality" can be further searched on the internet by using with standard practices of *http://www.google.com* and "keywords."

Astrophysics particles information reference:
The Large Hadron Collider (LHC)
The LHC is the largest machine in the world.
http://home.cern/topics/large-hadron-collider

Art frame warping, recoloring, differentiated editing was done by the book's author to all graphic work included.

Nonidentical artwork exists at any public domain sites that requires any graphics permissions.

NASA - National Aeronautics and Space Administration – Hubble Telescope

NASA web site content photo images. Web pages. Ref. https://www.nasa.gov/multimedia/guidelines/index.html

https://www.nasa.gov/mission_pages/hubble/main/index.html

WIKIPEDIA: No contract; nor any limited license.

Please make sure that you understand that the reference information provided here is being provided freely, and that no kind of agreement or contract is created between site users and/or the owners of WIKIPEDIA site. Use at your own risk.

Resources

Following is an abbreviated list of useful websites to do additional research on some of the topics covered in this new informative/educational metaphysics book for the intellectually curious reader.

http://www.google.com

https://en.wikipedia.org

https://math.berkeley.edu/~kwray/papers/string_theory.pdf

https://en.wikipedia.org/wiki/Sine_wave

https://en.wikipedia.org/wiki/Fractal sequence

http://home.cern/topics/large-hadron-collider

https://www.nasa.gov/mission_pages/hubble/main/index.html

royalty free clip art and graphics.org

https://www.publicdomainvectors.org

http://www.nbcnews.com/science/8-8-billion-habitable-earth-size-planets-exist-milky-way

https://www.amazon.com/

https://curiositystream.com/

http://superstringtheory.com/

https://www.khanacademy.org/science/physics/quantum-physics

Ref. https://www.nasa.gov/multimedia/guidelines/index.html

The Observer's Reality - Miscellaneous notes

Author's final Biniverse Graphics Theory notes:

I want to point out that the Biniverse Graph for energy – space – time theory shows the initial 1st Biniverse sinewave cycle as a symmetrical complete 360 degrees' loop ref. pages 111, and 116 with the present atomic converted matter of the universe around **5%** of the positive **Y** phase slope after 13.77 billion years past the initial Big-Bang point of 0 to 1 transition.

But when the combination of the remaining balance of ~95% hydrogen and the approx. 72% dark radiation energy combined with the ~23% dark matter does take the atomic biniverse to the peak of the positive **+Y** phase in about ~1.3 trillion years assuming a linear conversion for simplicity instead of a natural logarithmic scale as nature seems to prefer.

Then at that point *all bets are off*. The atomic universe may at that time be expanding close to the speed of light slowing time. All matter may force gravity to warp space into its own self-closing with space-time vanishing, and the peak of the atomic reality of existence vertically dropping into a non-symmetrical singularity point shown at the start of the sinewave cycle. Another possibility at that time is an expected vertical drop with a big crunch ending from the top of the Y phase to the bottom into the X phase cycle as a cosmos singularity.

This will reset the biniverse/universe for the next cycle, and a new unique cycle with different laws, and rules may start (Ref. to fig. 121 page 116), but always using energy as the driving sculpturing force, and main tool to carve the new Biniverse. RAZ Jr.

References

Charles Darwin (1809-1882) Theory of Evolution
Periodic Table of Elements: Dmitri Mendeleev By 1869, a total of 63 elements had been discovered. The Modern Periodic Table - The last major changes to the periodic table resulted from Glenn Seaborg's work in the middle of the 20th century. Starting with his discovery of plutonium in 1940, he discovered all the transuranic elements from 94 to 102. As of 2014, there were ~118 elements known to science. The most recently discovered super heavy element, *ununpentium* was confirmed in 2013 as atomic No. 115. Ref. page 48.

The Universe is quantized: Familiar quantities such as energy, momentum, electric charge, mass – possibly even time and space – are not continuous. They occur in discrete *quantum units*. This fact is not directly observable in day-to-day life because the intervals between the units are incredibly small.

Quantum Physics: The energy of electromagnetic radiation (light, radio waves, etc.) is transferred in discrete quantum packets called photons, and the energy of the photons is related to the frequency of the electromagnetic radiation by: $E=hf$, where h = *Planck's constant* = 6.63×10^{-34} J-sec Photons also carry momentum, even though they have no mass. This is given by the formula $p=E/c$.5) If we take the formulas given above for photons, and remember that light is a wave so it obeys $v = c = f\lambda$, we have: $p = E / c = hf / c = h / \lambda$ - Ref. Max Plank, Max Born, Erwin Schrodinger, Quantum physics equations. Ref. quantum mechanics https://www.khanacademy.org/science/physics/quantum-physics

References

Science cannot solve the ultimate mystery of nature. And that is because, in the last analysis, we ourselves are a part of the mystery that we are trying to solve. – Max Planck
http://faculty.wcas.northwestern.edu/~infocom/Ideas/qn_summary.pdf

Astronomical spectroscopy: The most easily-observed manifestation of quantum mechanics is the line spectra of excited gases. When an electric current is passed through a low-pressure gas, light comes off which, if viewed through a prism, can be seen to consist of discrete, narrow lines of color. The frequency of the light in these lines corresponds exactly (by $E = hf$) to the energy differences between the quantum levels in the atoms. Electrons "jumping" between levels can only give off (or absorb) photons whose energies are the same as the energy differences between the levels. Ref. Max Plank, Max Born, Erwin Schrodinger, Quantum physics equations. Ref. page 36

String Theory: String theory is a work in progress. The key string theory feature is that all objects in our universe are composed of vibrating filaments (strings) and membranes (branes) of energy. Several extra (usually unobservable) dimensions to the universe must exist. Ref. https://www.khanacademy.org/

Fractals: A rough or fragmented geometric shape that can be subdivided in parts, each of which is (at least approximately) a reduced/size copy of the whole. Ref. https://www.khanacademy.org/math/math-for-fun-and-glory/vi-hart/vi-cool-stuff/v/fractal-fractions

References

The Observer's Reality book references:

All topics, and subjects covered by this informative metaphysics book, "The Observer's Reality" can be further searched in the internet by using standard practices with *http://www.google.com* and "keywords."

Notes:

Given the present modern technology available for individuals to get reference links information, internet links are therefore no longer nowadays as mandatory of a requirement as much as it used to be, and in accordance the link list provided is limited due to lack of book space as a compromise to keep the size of this compact book.

Please try searching using: *http://www.google.com* with keywords as per ref. page 130

Book Author's P&V Database:

The book author has a large personal database with scientific information collected for over 25 years.

Most of the information used for "The Observer's Reality" metaphysics book project was extracted from the author's P&V Database fields of information contained within this personal software application, and was verified online during this project to be correct, and acceptable for the book's project. Ref. DB Fig. 114 at page 107.

Postface

Reader's additional information material

$$E = MC^2 \quad M = E/C^2 \quad C = \sqrt{E/M}$$

Albert Einstein Theory of Relativity which states that energy equals matter times speed of light squared.

Sinusoidal wave: A sinewave or sinusoid is a mathematical curve that describes a smooth repetitive oscillation. It is named after the function sine; of which it is the graph. It occurs often in pure and applied mathematics, as well as physics, engineering, signal processing and many other fields. Its most basic form as a function of time (t).
Ref. https://en.wikipedia.org/wiki/Sinewave

Fractal sequence: is one that contains itself as a proper subsequence. An example is: 1, 1, 2, 1, 2, 3, 1, 2, 3, 4, 1, 2, 3, 4, 5, 1, 2, 3, 4, 5, 6, ... If the first occurrence of each n is deleted, the remaining sequence is identical to the original. The process can be repeated indefinitely, so that the original sequence contains not only one copy of itself, but rather, infinitely many. Wikipedia

The precise definition of fractal sequence depends on a preliminary definition: a sequence $x = (x_n)$ is an infinitive sequence if for every i,

(F1) $x_n = i$ for infinitely many n.

Ref. https://en.wikipedia.org/wiki/Fractal_sequence

MTBF: Minimum time before failure caused by typical, and atypical wear, and tear that eventually will cause an expected calculated malfunction.

Appendix A

Algorithms Solution are the dynamic step-by-step repetitive automatic problem-solving procedures, incremental and established as recursive computational procedures for solving a problem in a finite number of repetitive incremental steps. Nature's laws are simple natural algorithms following energy conservation and efficiency fractals to improve a dynamic process using evolution.
https://www.khanacademy.org/computing/computer-science/algorithms

Binary Arithmetic first appeared in English in 1796 in a mathematical and philosophical dictionary. To represent numbers, the decimal system uses the powers of 10, whereas the binary system uses in a similar manner the powers of 2.
https://www.khanacademy.org/math/algebra-home/alg-intro-to-algebra/algebra-alternate-number

Binary System of numbers is the simplest of all positional number systems. The binary system works under the exact same principles as the decimal system, only it operates in base 2 rather than base 10. Instead of using the digits 0-9 as in the decimal system, Binary uses only 0-1 to perform all math. This is the language of computers. Ref. Gottfried W. Leibniz

Biniverse: Ref. Binary Graph - Energy – Space Time–by which the author's theory showing the possibility of a quantum oscillating biniverse at which we maybe living in the universe side with positive atomic matter at an off-phase atomic reality frequency of existence in a cyclic universe presently at a ~13.7 billion of this ongoing present binary **+Y** sinewave cycle. Fig. 2

Appendix B

Chaos theory principle (Ref. The Butterfly Effect) is the science of the nonlinear and the unpredictable nature's phenomena. Many natural objects exhibit fractal properties, including landscapes, clouds, trees, organs, and rivers. Recognizing the chaotic, fractal nature of our universe can give us new insight, power, wisdom, and enlightenment to understand true reality. Ref. https://www.youtube.com/watch?v=JnlkKdDXk- Chaos Theory video.

Darwin/Darwinism is a theory of biological life evolution that was developed by the English naturalist Charles Darwin (1809-1882) and others. It states that all species of organisms arise and develop through the natural selection of small, inherited variations that increase the individual's ability to compete, survive, and reproduce. Ref. http://www.darwins-theory-of-evolution.com/

Divinity & Spirituality as part of religion in some form or another has been around since the evolution of early man. The following are the major world religions and the number of believers in the world today: **Christianity** = ~2 billion or ~32%; **Islam** = ~1.57 billion or ~22%; **Hinduism** = ~950 million or ~13%; **Buddhism** = ~800 million or ~6%; **Atheists or Agnostic** (secularists) = ~900 million or ~15%; **Other religions** = less than 50 million each or ~1% for each different religion or faith. Ref. page 68. And priming information previous to **Chapter VII**.

Ref. Chapter VIII.
http://bulletin.hds.harvard.edu/articles/winterspring2010/spiritual-not-religious

Appendix C

Emergence is a process whereby larger entities arise through interactions among smaller or simpler entities, such that the larger entities exhibit properties the smaller/simpler entities do not show. For instance, the phenomenon of existing biological life is an emergent property of chemistry. The process of emergence is central in theories of integrative levels and complex systems. Ref. Chapter VI.

Fractals are a never-ending pattern. Fractals are infinitely complex patterns that are self-similar across different scales. They are created by repeating a simple process over and over in an ongoing feedback loop. http://fractalfoundation.org/videos/

Life & death is an emergent existence as a biological binary organized process controlled by energy efficiency use.
Ref. http://necsi.edu/guide/concepts/emergence.html

The Law of Probability: Probability measures the likelihood of an event or chance; odds occurring expressed mathematically. Ref.
https://www.probabilitycourse.com/chapter1/1_4_2_total_probability.php

Quantum Physics/String Theory: is a potential "theory of everything", uniting all matter and forces in a single theoretical framework, which describes the fundamental level of the universe in terms of vibrating strings rather than particles. Ref.
http://superstringtheory.com/
 https://www.google.com/
 https://curiositystream.com/

Book keywords

All topics, and subjects covered by this informative metaphysics book, "The Observer's Reality" can be further researched on the internet by using standard search computer practices using *http://www.google.com* and the following randomly-listed "keywords" ....

Algorithms Solution
Astrophysics
Brain
Biology
Binary Arithmetic
The Binary System
CERN
Chaos theory principle
Cosmology
Cancer cells
Chromosomes
Darwin/Darwinism
DNA – RNA
Emergence
Evolution
Fractals
NASA
Neuroethology
Particles
Periodic Table of Elements
Proteins
The Law of Probability
Quantum Mechanics
Quantum Physics
String Theory
Universe / Biniverse

Index

Albert Einstein, 3, 21, 31, 51, 57, 58, 98, 113, 116, 126
Amino acids, 51, 60, 61, 63, 97
Atoms, 22, 25, 32, 34, 35, 37, 38, 44, 47, 48, 51, 57, 109, 110, 113, 115, 124
Atomic energy, 25, 34, 90

Bacteria, 57
Biniverse, 3, 7, 10 to 16, 21, 22, 26, 30, 31, 32, to 41, 44 to 51, 64, 84, 88, 90, 93, 95, 98, 99, 101 to 106, 116
Black hole, 32, 33, 39, 43, 49, 95
Binary, 10, 11, 20, 12, 15, 21, 22, 23, 25, 27, 29, 31, 32, 33, 34, 35, 39, 40, 41, 44, 57, 58, 64, 69, 81, 87, 89, 90, 91, 93, 98, 99, 100, 104, 106, 108, 112, 113, 117, 119, 127, 129, 130

Carbon, 44, 49, 59, 60, 84, 85, 95, 96, 102, 110, 112, 115
Cancer, 17, 62, 109,
Cells, 13, 18, 56, 59, 60, 61, 62, 63. 67. 73, 75, 78, 85, 86, 87, 88, 89, 94, 95, 96, 97, 102, 103, 109, 112, 130

Chaos, 12, 22, 26, 32, 34, 37, 40, 58, 71, 93, 98, 109, 128, 130
Chromosomes, 12, 60, 61, 63, 87, 97, 130
Chemical elements, 84
Chess, 13, 92, 93
DNA, 8, 10, 12, 13, 17, 18, 49, 53, 56, 60, 61, 62, 63, 84, 85, 87, 88, 97, 103, 110, 130
Duality, 23, 29, 33, 34, 112

Earth, 7, 11, 16, 25, 27, 28, 38, 39, 40, 41, 43, 44, 45, 46, 47, 49, 50, 51, 52, 54, 56, 57, 59, 63, 65, 73, 86, 89, 90, 91, 92, 97, 100, 102, 103, 110, 112, 113, 115, 121

Electrons, 37, 91, 124
Electro-magnetic, 51, 112
Emergence, 22, 31, 32, 34, 44, 51, 57, 80, 86, 87, 104, 106, 113, 117, 129, 130

Index

Environmental, 23, 54, 63, 65, 77, 103
Evolution, 11, 12, 14, 17, 23, 27, 43, 45, 47, 49, 51, 52, 56 to 65, 69. 70, 71, 73, 76, 81, 84, 86, 88, 89, 93, 98, 106, 109, 127, 128, 130
Faith, 27, 68, 71, 104, 105, 128
Galaxy, 2, 10, 11, 12, 25, 28, 38, 40 to 45, 50, 69, 112, 113
Genes, 60, 61, 62, 63, 67, 71, 76, 88, 89
Genetic, 23, 54, 63, 67, 78, 82, 92, 97, 101, 106
Gravity, 41, 43, 49, 56, 99, 102, 112, 113

Humans, 17, 27, 28, 46, 57, 59, 63, 66, 84, 87, 93, 96. 102, 103, 112

Infinity, 69, 108
Intellectual, 28, 76, 80, 81, 101
Intelligence, 62, 69, 76, 82, 102

Jupiter, 41, 113

Kinetic energy, 112

Light, 13, 21, 26, 40, 41, 43, 47, 51, 52, 56, 58, 68, 69, 86, 94, 105, 108, 112, 113, 123, 124, 126, 128
Light year, 40, 41, 102
Living organisms, 17, 23, 52, 60, 70, 85, 86, 88, 89

Milky Way, 2, 10, 11, 25, 28, 40, 41, 42, 45, 49, 50, 112, 113
Molecules, 12, 44, 51, 56, 60, 62, 63, 85, 97, 110, 115
Matter, 7, 11, 21, 22, 26, 32, 33, 34, 35, 37, 38, 39, 41, 45, 51, 58, 60, 70, 71, 81, 98, 100, 103, 104, 109, 110
Metals, 95
Metaphysics, 4, 5, 27, 29, 35, 59, 80, 81, 99, 100, 104, 106, 107, 109, 110, 120, 121, 125, 130
Neurons, 13, 62, 74, 78, 94, 97
Negative, 21, 31, 32, 35, 41, 58, 105, 112
Nuclear, 26, 37, 38, 53, 56, 98, 102, 112

Index

Orbits, 43, 113

Planets, 7, 11, 26, 27, 38, 39, 40, 41, 43, 49, 50, 57, 103, 112, 113, 121

Probability, 16, 21, 23, 27, 29, 31, 34, 35, 41, 45, 54, 57, 63, 106, 108, 110, 129, 130

Protein, 12, 13, 49, 53, 60, 61, 62, 63, 84, 85, 97, 110
Particles, 10, 14, 22, 25, 26, 34, 35, 37, 38, 43, 60, 75, 91, 99, 108, 109, 113, 117, 120, 129

Quantum Theory, 91, 130, 134
Quantum Physics, 16, 22, 23, 32, 34, 99, 100, 109, 123, 124, 129

Relativity, 3, 21, 31, 37, 38, 51, 58, 68, 98, 104, 113, 116, 126

Solar system, 7, 11, 25, 26, 27, 38, 39, 40, 41, 43, 45, 50, 112, 113
Sun, 28, 38, 40, 41, 43, 44, 49, 50, 52, 56, 86, 102, 112, 113
Stars, 22, 32, 37 to 45, 49, 50, 84, 89, 96, 112, 113
Supernova, 39, 43, 49, 50, 84
Stem Cells, 60, 97

Theory, 3, 7, 12, 14, 16, 21, 23, 25, 31, 37, 38, 51, 58, 64, 68, 71, 86, 90, 91, 98, 104, 108, 112, 113, 116, 117, 119, 121, 123, 124, 126, 127
Thesis, 25, 27, 28, 52, 80, 85, 88, 86, 109
Time-Space, 55

Universal, 8, 13, 23, 26, 33, 40, 43, 45, 47, 49, 50, 56, 57, 65, 69, 71, 81, 84, 87, 88, 89, 91, 95, 96, 104, 110, 112
Universal law, 71, 104

Virus, 13, 17, 89

Wave, 31, 33, 35, 74, 90, 91, 110, 111, 112, 113, 119, 121, 123, 126

X-Ray, 29

Zapathousky, 13

The Observer's Reality book
Sources & Art credits

Copyright information: NASA web site content photo images, or data in any format - *Are generally not copyrighted.* As per NASA, you may use this material for educational or informational purposes, including photo collections. This general permission extends to personal Web pages. Ref. – Graphics credits.
Ref. https://www.nasa.gov/multimedia/guidelines/index.html

Art frame warping, recoloring, differentiated editing was done by the book's author to all graphic work included.

Nonidentical artwork exists at any public domain sites that requires any graphics permissions.

Disclaimer: Be aware that this informative and educational metaphysics book does not contain pictorials, photos, or attachments from any free royalty public domain websites. But hereby also be notified that before taking any commercial actions for monetary purposes based on any of the enclosed book material, artwork documentation, and, or enclosed book information. It should be verified to properly comply, and be authorized by the respective author if required.

Ref. *royalty free clip art and graphics.org* - publicdomainvectors.org
And many other *royalty free clip art and graphics* websites etc.

WIKIPEDIA: No contract; nor any limited license.

Please make sure that you understand that the reference information provided here is being provided freely, and that no kind of agreement or contract is created between site users and/or the owners of WIKIPEDIA site. Use at your own risk.

Printed by: CreateSpace, An Amazon.com Company
• Available from Amazon.com and other retail outlets
ISBN-13: 9780692866856

About the Author

No. 125 - The Observer's Reality

I worked for a total of 23 years in R&D Eng. Dept. biomedical new scientific instruments product development of medical clinical and hospital auto hematology blood cell counters, multi-parameters analyzers of blood cells using lasers, high radio frequency sonar, and D.C. impedance for characterization and particle analyzers used in-vitro biomedical hospital, and clinical

No. 126 Skull - E*xit the brain trip now...* - Diag. labs.

5 years in R&D Elect. Eng. - **No. 127 – PCB Design** working for an European Aviation Co. in avionics instrumentation as an EE. I also hold an airplane commercial multi-engine instrument FAA pilot license.

I worked another 10 years for a Japanese Medical Diagnostic Company in the R&D Eng. Dept. as an electrical engineer in biomedical glucose meters' diabetes technology. ***Ref. Above Glucose Meter PCB Design.***

Working with very complex new electronic circuit schematics, multi-layer surface mount printed circuit boards was a part of my life in Eng. R&D for many years.

I am broadly interested in physics, neuroscience, Elect. engineering, biology, astrophysics, neurology and the applications of these fields in biomedical medicine.

This book became a project I contemplated doing for when I get the time needed to try to reverse engineer our own human design, and some of the universe auto-creation existence, and the mysteries for which I wanted to find possible optional answers.

Author's Notes

I hope that you enjoyed the myriad of information, art, photos, and illustrations I put together in a compact way for your learning pleasure.

Ref. $E=MC^2$ or $M = E/C^2$ and $C = \sqrt{E/M}$

I will like to ask the readers for your feedback on my 1st book. Writing a book is a real challenge and I made my share of amateur errors during this task; most of which I hope were corrected. I thank you for your patience and understanding for any errors left undetected at the time of the final publication.

Your comments and any positive or even negative constructive criticism, suggestions, and/or any ideas that were left out from *"The Observer's Reality"* will be appreciated to my e-mail: hyperspace@comcast.net

<u>Thank you</u>! & Best regards,

RAZ Jr. - Published author

"The Observer's Reality"
A Metaphysics book
where the mystery of true reality is solved........

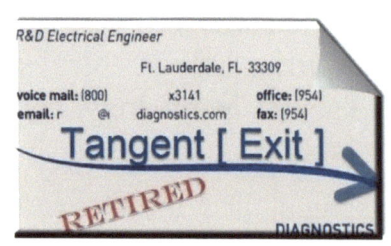

Book Publication - 2017

Brain decoded encrypted words:

The brain has the capacity to find or decode missing information, and find solutions by integrating existing memories, and knowledge to find required unknown solutions. I like the observer metaphysics book a lot so far. (Ref. page 77 solution).

The Observer's Reality

Red white platelet processor prototype card for a hospital grade Auto Blood Cell Analyzer. Ref. fig. 80 - page 82.

Microcomputer radio transceiver PCB with GPS & Bluetooth® design done by book's author consultant job after retirement.

Remember to live only in the present.
It is a once in a lifetime unique gift.
The past is gone and the future is not guaranteed.

By: RAZ Jr.

THE END

www.ingramcontent.com/pod-product-compliance
Lightning Source LLC
Chambersburg PA
CBHW041614220426
43670CB00001B/11